TRIPS ON WHEELS

15 Driving Tours from the Front Range

by
Leslie Bergstrom

Illustrated by
Cyndy Wacker

DEDICATION

This book is dedicated to the
Glory of God
and
to my friends and colleagues
in
Tailored Tours of Colorado Springs

First printing, September 1985

ACKNOWLEDGEMENTS

Several years of working with information on Colorado Springs, the United States Air Force Academy, Cripple Creek, Canon City, and Denver have given the author a backlog of knowledge in those areas. Repeated family vacations to Aspen and Glenwood Springs made that tour second nature. However, many new places presented themselves in the course of working on TRIPS ON WHEELS, and many people helped in its completion.

Particular thanks go to the following, who assisted me in starting research:

Thelma Carneal — Monument and Palmer Lake
Milt Mathis — Calhan
Barbara Martin — La Junta
Paulette Moore — Pueblo
Evelyn Ely — Westcliffe
The senior citizens "lunch bunch" — Silver Cliff

Membership in the Colorado Historical Society proved invaluable, especially because of its publications, the monthly newsletter and the quarterly *Colorado Heritage* magazine.

Thanks to Leland Feitz, Vivian McWhorter, Judie Werschky, and Rhoda Wilcox for reading the manuscript, making suggestions and corrections, and offering only encouragement and positive criticism.

Most special thanks to my daughter, Kim, and my husband, Jim. Kim, co-author of TRIPS ON TWOS, always knew exactly where I was headed with TRIPS ON WHEELS even when I took a detour, broke down or lost my way. Jim chauffeured and shared on many exploratory trips that covered hundreds of miles.

TABLE OF CONTENTS

MAPS   **Page**

Colorado 6
Colorado Springs 8
Foothills — Three Trips on Wheels North 21
United States Air Force Academy....................... 27
Tri-Lakes, Black Forest 27
Denver 36
Denver Downtown 40
High Plains — One Trip on Wheels East 48
Rivers and Valleys — Five Trips on Wheels South 55
Pueblo 63
Wet Mountain Valley — Canon City 69
Trinidad.. 79
Cuchara Valley....................................... 80
San Luis Valley....................................... 80
Mountains — Five Trips on Wheels West 87
Rocky Mountain National Park 90
Aspen.. 98
Where the Mines Were 103
Leadville 111
Cripple Creek 118

FOREWORD 7
TOUR 1   COLORADO SPRINGS 9
              North 11
              East 13
              South 16
              West 19

FOOTHILLS — THREE TRIPS ON WHEELS NORTH
TOUR 2   UNITED STATES AIR FORCE ACADEMY 22
TOUR 3   TRI-LAKES 28
              Black Forest
              Woodmoor
              Palmer Lake
              Glen Park
              Monument
TOUR 4   DENVER................................... 34
              Route 1..................................... 36
              Downtown.................................. 39
              Route 2..................................... 43

HIGH PLAINS — ONE TRIP ON WHEELS EAST
TOUR 5   HIGH PLAINS 47
              Option — Franktown
                         Castlewood Canyon State Park
                         Elizabeth, Elbert
              Tour   — Calhan 49
                         Paint Mines
                         Ellicott

RIVERS AND VALLEYS — FIVE TRIPS ON WHEELS SOUTH
TOUR 6   ARKANSAS VALLEY 56
          Rocky Ford, Swink
          Bent's Old Fort National Historic Site
          La Junta
TOUR 7   PUEBLO 61
TOUR 8   WET MOUNTAIN VALLEY — CANON CITY 67
          Wetmore
          Silver Cliff, Westcliffe
          Royal Gorge
TOUR 9   CUCHARA VALLEY — TRINIDAD 74
          La Veta
          Cuchara
TOUR 10   SAN LUIS VALLEY 81
          San Luis
          Fort Garland
          Great Sand Dunes National Monument
          Crestone

MOUNTAINS — FIVE TRIPS ON WHEELS WEST
TOUR 11   ROCKY MOUNTAIN NATIONAL PARK 88
          Estes Park
          Grand Lake
          Winter Park
TOUR 12   ASPEN — GLENWOOD SPRINGS 95
          Independence Pass
          Maroon Bells
          Vail
TOUR 13   WHERE THE MINES WERE 101
          Golden
          Black Hawk, Central City, Idaho Springs
          Georgetown, Silver Plume
          Breckenridge
          Alma, Fairplay
TOUR 14   LEADVILLE 110
          Buena Vista
          Climax
          Twin Lakes
TOUR 15   CRIPPLE CREEK 117
          Manitou Springs
          Ute Pass
          Victor
          Florissant Fossil Beds National Monument

A COLORADO READING LIST 124

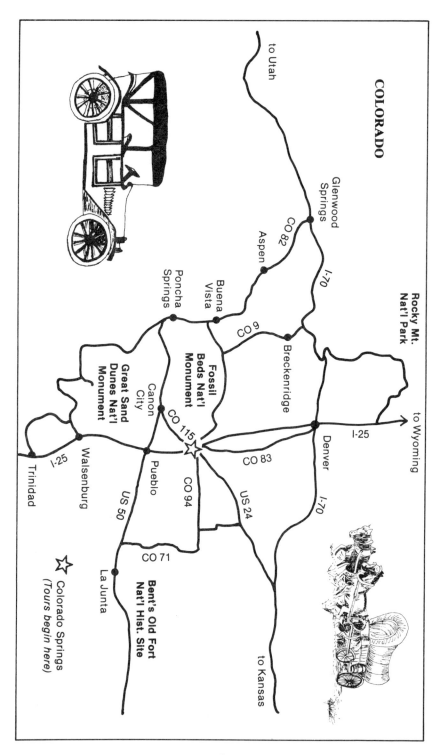

COLORADO

Rocky Mt.
Nat'l Park

to Utah

Glenwood
Springs

CO 82

Aspen

I-70

Poncha
Springs

Buena
Vista

CO 9

Breckenridge

Fossil
Beds Nat'l
Monument

Great Sand
Dunes Nat'l
Monument

Canon
City

CO 115

to Wyoming

I-25

Denver

I-70

CO 83

US 24

Trinidad

I-25

Walsenburg

Pueblo

CO 94

US 50

to Kansas

CO 71

La Junta

☆ Colorado Springs
(Tours begin here)

Bent's Old Fort
Nat'l Hist. Site

6

FOREWORD

Welcome to Colorado adventures and to a book that presents dozens of ideas on how to enjoy our beautiful state! Find a variety of themes sprinkled throughout the pages. Trace the story of Native Americans, plus that of emigrants and immigrants from various states and nations. Explore with United States Army topographic engineers. Follow trappers and traders, settlers and goldseekers, and modern space-age pioneers. Watch the business development of mines and of railroads, the manufacturing of steel and of microcomputer chips.

Experience geography, geology, flora, and fauna as you journey from arid plains to forested peaks, from sand dunes to mountain streams. Pass through five of the six life zones in North America, a journey equal to one from Mexico to Alaska, as you climb from prairie to timberline.

TRIPS ON WHEELS is designed to stand alone or as a companion volume to TRIPS ON TWOS. The latter, a book of walking tours, provides far more detailed information on Colorado Springs, Manitou Springs and the United States Air Force Academy.

Colorado Springs' central location on the Front Range makes it the perfect spot to use as a headquarters and a jumping-off point for all the tours. However, you may enjoy the trips from any Eastern Slope city; simply modify the routes and the estimated driving times.

In addition to this foreward, other prefaces appear before each section of tours. Preceding each trip find the author's personal comments and suggestions set in *italics* and the historic introduction set in **bold face**. The tours are set in larger type, with special options and clarifications in *italics*.

A criterion in organizing the tours was to present trips that you can complete in a single day, albeit a long one in some cases. But it's better to have a brief acquaintance with delightful destinations than not to go at all! Many of the tours cry for more than one day, however, and several can be strung together if you have more time. See specific suggestions in each section.

In most cases the trips are circle tours, usually planned so that after a busy day you return on the best highway. Only infrequently will you be retracing the same itinerary.

Wide open stretches present themselves on many of the trips so be prepared. Fill your gas tank before starting. Take maps, sunglasses, water, food, and jackets as Colorado weather can change rapidly. Picnics save time and allow you a chance to enjoy the countryside. Binoculars and books to identify birds, trees and flowers will enhance your journeys.

The information given here is as up to date as possible, but unfortunately, in Colorado today's open space is tomorrow's development, and this year's attraction may have changed hands or closed down by next year. Expansion creates new roads, modifies old ones and paves dirt ones.

Spring weather can be capricious, but the season brings wildflowers and baby animals. Summer offers the benefits of long daylight hours and open attractions, but you must compete with many other travelers. Fall presents aspen colors and bright blue skies. And don't dismiss winter in the high country—a special time of delight. With your TRIPS ON WHEELS as a guide and companion, take off in any direction at any time of year to savor the wonder that is Colorado!

7

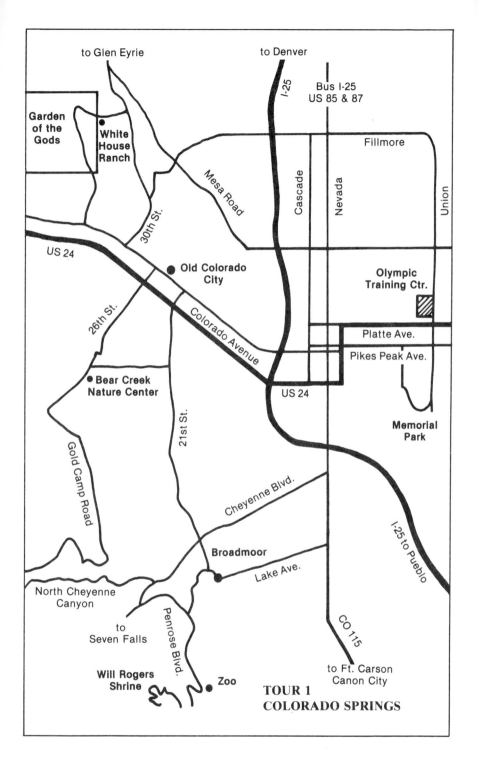

TOUR 1
COLORADO SPRINGS

COLORADO SPRINGS

Previewing the rest of the trips, the tour of Colorado Springs divides into North, East, South, and West sections. You can put the segments together, use them individually, or even let them begin tours out of town in the same direction. For example, the North section can join the Air Force Academy tour; East can precede the High Plains; South leads in to either Pueblo or Canon City; West takes you to Cripple Creek.

You will enjoy your tour more if you stop occasionally for a short walk. To enhance your exploration of Colorado Springs, incorporate the information found in TRIPS ON TWOS. Also consider two more short walks. Begin at the Hearthstone Inn, walk one block north, turn right and circle the block. Take a little stroll along Cascade and/or Wood Avenues, particularly the 1400 and 1500 blocks on Wood.

At the end of the tour find the option to visit Glen Eyrie Castle, General Palmer's magnificent home. You must first telephone The Navigators to ascertain times for guided tours or when you may drive through the grounds.

Mileage: 40 miles　　　　　　　　　　*Actual driving time: 1½ hours*

People make history, and the history of Colorado Springs reflects many personalities. Tourists and invalids, railroad tycoons and mining nabobs, military personnel and high technology wizards, in turn all came to Pikes Peak, liked what they saw, stayed and added new chapters to the region's colorful story.

General William Jackson Palmer of Pennsylvania, experienced railroad man and veteran of the Civil War, became one of the great builders of the West. A man of courage, foresight and generosity, he founded both Colorado Springs and the Denver and Rio Grande Railroad in 1871. While many Colorado communities came about because of a specific need, such as serving the mines, Colorado Springs developed as a desirable location to which people would want to come for its own sake.

And come they did! Even in the raw early years adventurous travelers from the East and from Europe enjoyed the glorious scenery and healthy outdoor life. In the decade of the 1880s, villas sprang up in the North End, Colorado College provided a cultural focus, and the finest hotel in the Rockies welcomed tourists.

In addition to the vacationers, other visitors came chasing good health. Doctors sent tuberculars, also called "consumptives" or "lungers," here as a last resort. Many recovered in the clear sunshine and pure mountain air to spend long and productive lives devoted to the city in which they found the cure. Sanatoria stretched from Cragmoor by northeast Austin's Bluffs to Montcalme at the base of the mountains in Manitou. The curative powers of Manitou's mineral springs,

9

known first to the Indians centuries before settlers came, also contributed to the region's fame as a health mecca.

Colorado Springs developed into a great railroad town. Palmer's Denver and Rio Grande and James J. Hagerman's Colorado Midland led the way. Eventually seven different railroads served the city. Several blocks separated the D&RG depot to the west and the Santa Fe station to the east. The unwary traveler had to be careful; southbound trains departed from one station and northbound trains from the other.

To some members of the entrenched society of Colorado Springs, the discovery of gold almost in their back yard seemed slightly vulgar, but many citizens flocked to Cripple Creek. The transition from mountain cattle ranch to the world's richest gold camp spanned the decade of the 1890s.

The Midas-like success of her first thirty years carried Colorado Springs well into the twentieth century. The impetus slowed with World War I, slumped between the wars, and swelled once again in the World War II years. The new bonanza came dressed in a military uniform. Colorado Springs provides acreage for the army's Fort Carson, Peterson Air Force Base, the United States Air Force Academy, the North American Aerospace Defense Command, and the Consolidated Space Operations Center.

As a vibrant space age city Colorado Springs also plays host to a swelling number of high technology industries. Drawn by the low humidity, business environment, military installations, and a winning quality of life and recreation, some of the country's most sophisticated technological businesses have moved to the Pikes Peak Region. Hewlitt-Packard, first of the companies to locate here, arrived in 1962. A whole new electronics vocabulary joins those of tourism, medicine, railroads, mining, and military in the latest Colorado Springs boom.

Begin this tour at the corner of Pikes Peak and Cascade Avenues in downtown Colorado Springs. Note the Antlers Hotel and the Holly Sugar Building in Chase Stone Center.

The present hotel is the third Antlers at this site. The first opened in 1883 and reigned as the most fashionable hostelry in the Rocky Mountain West until fire destroyed the building in 1898. Three years later the second Antlers provided modern and elegant accommodations and served the city's guests until its demolition in 1964.

The successful raising of sugar beets in Colorado sparked an industry to process the brown root vegetable. Growing began in the 1860s and the first processing factory appeared in 1899. A $3 million industry developed by 1901, and 1909 saw 79,000 Colorado acres planted to sugar beets. Founded in 1905, Holly Sugar Corporation became the nation's third largest beet sugar producer.

Drive south to the end of Chase Stone Center and turn right on Antlers Place. Pass the south side of Antlers Park and turn right along its west side. See the old railroad station on the left and Engine 168 of the Denver and Rio Grande on the right. Make a small jog to continue straight ahead up the hill to a right on Kiowa, a one-way street headed east, and prepare to turn left on Cascade.

Look to your left as you reach Kiowa to view St. Mary's Basilica. Worship began at this site in 1891, and 1907 saw the completion of towers and steeples.

To your right note Penrose Library. Mining millionaire Spencer Penrose built the Broadmoor Hotel and established charitable El Pomar Foundation with his fortune. The library commemorates Penrose and his wife, Julie.

As you turn left on Cascade, glance right to see the Latvian Freedom Fountain. Latvian refugees, over one hundred strong, financed the memorial to their lost independence.

Hearthstone Inn

☙ NORTH ❧

Drive north on Cascade to the 400 block. On the right stands McAllister House Museum, a Victorian cottage with red brick walls twenty inches thick. General Palmer brought Major Henry McAllister west to supervise the land company responsible for developing Colorado Springs. The home's interior features authentic period furniture and the skilled carpentry work of Winfield Scott Stratton, who later struck it very rich in Cripple Creek.

Diagonally across Cascade see Hearthstone Inn, a bed and breakfast establishment and former home of the Judson Bemis family. Bemis's

11

fortune from an Ohio paper bag company financed construction of the 1885 dwelling. His daughter, Alice Bemis Taylor, contributed funds for the Colorado Springs Fine Arts Center. The old carriage house joins the corner inn to its companion, once a TB sanatorium.

Author Frank Waters wrote about his grandfather, Joseph Dozier. Dozier served as contractor for the Bemis house and for another 1885 mansion at 610 North Cascade. James J. Hagerman, who built the Colorado Midland Railway to reach mountain mines and quarries, invested $30,000 in this massive stone house.

Continue north one and one-half blocks to Dale Street. Locate the Colorado Springs Fine Arts Center to your left partway down the hill. The exterior of reinforced concrete recalls southwestern pueblo architecture, while the interior features Art Deco furnishings. A building for all the arts, the Center includes galleries, theater, music room, and museum shop.

The American Numismatic Association occupies Colorado College property at 810 North Cascade. The ANA's museum galleries exhibit coins, currencies and medals from classical to contemporary issues. World mints supply models of medallions for the hands-on gallery, Hall of Nations, in the rotunda.

The main portion of Colorado College's campus extends from Cache la Poudre to San Rafael Streets. The oldest structure on the campus, 1880 Cutler Hall, stands west of Cascade. General Palmer reserved acreage for the college when Colorado Springs began, and its opening in 1874 made it the first college or university in the Rockies.

As the 1880s drew to a close, building of the great homes moved from north of downtown to north of Colorado College. The 1889 house at 1130 North Cascade typifies the brick and stone construction once prevalent in the area. Use of the cylindrical tower in a variety of building materials and sizes became a trademark of local architecture.

Crossing Uintah Street puts one in the extensive Old North End Historic District, created in 1983. The eclectic mixture of architectural styles and the personalities of their owners — society visitors and recovered invalids, millionaires from Cripple Creek and professional people — stamp their character on the Old North End.

Enjoy the wealth of historical dwellings as you proceed north on Cascade seven blocks to Fontanero. Turn left and left again onto Wood Avenue. Named for D. Russ Wood, who developed the Wood Subdivision, blocks of the avenue north of Colorado College carried the title "Millionaire Row."

On the southeast corner of Wood and Fontanero, northern boundary of the historic Wood Subdivision, stands the former home of the Alexander brothers. Charles Lindbergh considered an Alexander Aircraft plane for his transatlantic flight. By 1950 the Alexander Film Company was making daily shipments of 16,000 feet of advertising film to theaters across the country and around the world.

In the 1500 block begins a concentration of turn-of-the-century homes and a series of decorative iron fences produced by the Hassell Iron Works of Colorado City. On the northeast corner of Wood and San Miguel find "The Showplace of Millionaire Row," home of plumber Jimmie Burns, who became a Cripple Creek mining mogul. On the southwest corner of Wood and Uintah lived the Wood brothers (not to be confused with D. Russ) whose fortune came from Victor gold.

Turn right on Uintah, drive downhill across Monument Creek and turn left on Glen. On your left appears the original Van Briggle Art Pottery Building.

At the Louvre young Artus Van Briggle spotted Ming Dynasty pots with a silky, "dead glaze" matte finish. His goal became to rediscover and reproduce the art, and Van Briggle's experiments proved successful. His prize-winning Art Nouveau pottery first captured international attention at the Paris Exposition of 1901. Following his death from TB at age 35, his widow, Anne, planned this building as a memorial. General Palmer donated the land, and Anne designed and made the decorative exterior tiles.

Continue south on Glen past memorial peony and iris beds and Willow Pond. Reach the Demonstration Garden at the next corner. Volunteer horticulturalists maintain a variety of plantings throughout the growing season.

Turn left, cross the bridge over Monument Creek and take the road to the left up the hill. Reach Tejon Street and turn right. The turn-of-the-century Plaza Building appears on your right. Look for several historic churches along Tejon, some of the houses of worship that gave Colorado Springs the designation "City of Churches."

Arrive at Platte Avenue. On your right note the red brick El Paso Club, begun as the first private men's club west of Chicago. Turn left and drive along the north side of Acacia Park.

ⳇ⳥ EAST ⳇ⳥

The bronze equestrian statue of General William Jackson Palmer, founder of Colorado Springs, stands frozen in its stride at Platte and Nevada Avenues. True to tradition regarding Civil War generals, as a northern officer General Palmer faces south. His head turns to view his beloved mountains.

At the next corner, Weber Street, turn left and drive six blocks past some Victorian restorations. Note the stylish renovations as bright paint hues, coordinating with colorful roof treatments, hopscotch from house to house. Reflecting an era in which more was considered better, the houses contain towers, turrets, cupolas, porches, carpentry and carving details, decorative shingles, and a variety of window shapes.

Until recently many old homes carried the aura of a gentlewoman fallen on hard times, garbed in faded elegance and frayed lace. Enactment of a federal law in 1979 encouraged contractors to tackle renovations with low-interest loans. In many cases the new facelifts involve both exterior renewal and interior remodeling.

Continue to Cache La Poudre Street; turn right and proceed four blocks east. Observe that many smaller homes also have welcomed the painter's touch. Drive under the old Santa Fe Railroad overpass, continue one more block to Prospect Street and turn right. Go two blocks to Franklin Street, turn right and follow the curve of the road along Shook's Run Park to continue south on El Paso Street.

A pleasant green belt close to downtown, Shook's Run Park parallels a meandering creek of the same name and the AT&SF railroad bed, where a paved bike path and walking trail replaces the former tracks.

Turn right on Bijou Street past more houses of the Victorian persuasion. The home at 435 East Bijou housed the grandparents of Winfield Scott Stratton's biographer, Frank Waters. Waters' grandfather, Joseph Dozier, served as contractor for such buildings as the Hearthstone Inn and the Hagerman House on North Cascade and Cutler Hall at Colorado College.

Go left at Wahsatch Avenue, drive one block and turn left again onto Kiowa. On both sides of the street take in the constantly changing collection of architectural styles and building materials — everything from brick and stone to clapboard and shingle, from small cottage to three-story Victorian. Hopa crabapple trees add a burst of color in the spring.

Kiowa deadends into the grounds of the Colorado School for the Deaf and Blind. General Palmer gave the original ten-acre tract for the state institution, organized in 1874.

Turn right at Institute Street for one block, then left at Pikes Peak Avenue. Continue east on Pikes Peak and note Memorial Park on your right. Be prepared to turn right into the park four blocks east of the traffic light on Hancock, opposite Farragut Street on the left.

Memorial Park contains facilities for a variety of sports, including baseball, softball, ice skating, and swimming. Holiday weekends are big events in the park. The Fourth of July presents day-long festivities capped by a performance of the Colorado Springs Symphony Orchestra, Fort Carson cannons and fireworks. Labor Day weekend welcomes the Colorado Springs Balloon Classic, a major annual event for hot air balloonists.

Follow the park's main road with the center yellow line as it turns left at the yield sign and curves past the ice rink and the pool. On the left lies the Velodrome, completed in the summer of 1983 for the fifth annual National Sports Festival. A world record fell at this site in 1984 while selecting the men's cycling team for the Summer Olympics. On the right a war memorial honors U.S. servicemen.

Turn left at the stop sign on Union Boulevard. Across the street stand the headquarters of the International Typographic Union and the Union Printers Home. The 1891 Home recalls Colorado Springs' history as a medical resort. The local Board of Trade donated a 246-acre tract, and the Home was self-sustaining with dairy cattle, hogs and chickens. Formal flower beds allowed tuberculars to stroll through pleasant surroundings while enjoying mountain air and sunshine. An early streetcar line from Colorado Springs made a loop in front of the Home before returning to downtown.

After the 1976 Olympic Games officials decided to establish a national training center, and the United States Olympic Committee moved its headquarters to Colorado Springs in 1977. Occupying the former site of Ent Air Force Base and the then North American Air Defense Command, the city-owned property rents to the USOC at one dollar per year. High altitude training provides an added bonus for athletes.

The 34-acre facility can accommodate up to 550 athletes at one time. The highly sophisticated, ultra-modern sports medicine program features the most advanced laboratories in the country to monitor sports physiology and biomechanics.

Stop at the gatehouse for information and continue on a self-guided tour of the premises.

Greeting visitors immediately inside the gate is the circle of flags representing the national governing boards for sports included in the Olympic Games. West of the flags stand the five Olympic rings and Olympic House. The National Sports Building formerly headquartered NORAD, now located in Cheyenne Mountain. To the north find the Sports Medicine Building, Sports Center, training areas, track, and dormitories. Note that building names within the complex recall the sites of former Olympic Games.

Leave the Olympic Training Complex and turn right. Drive west on Boulder to reach Nevada Avenue and turn left.

౭ఆౖ SOUTH ౭ఆౖ

Pass General Palmer's statue and Acacia Park. At the corner of Nevada and Kiowa find Colorado Springs City Hall on the left and the Colorado Springs Company Building on the right. At the corner of Pikes Peak Avenue note the Mining Exchange Building (once the world's busiest) on the right.

Turn right at Colorado Avenue past the City Administration Building. In one block turn left on Tejon Street. On each side of the street stand the modern red brick structures which complement the historic Alamo Building on the right at the next corner. See the Pioneers Museum to the left, housed in the former El Paso County Courthouse. The museum provides an excellent introduction to all facets of Pikes Peak Country's history.

Continue on Tejon past south-of-town renovations. On the northeast corner of Rio Grande Street stands the Old English style Colorado Springs Day Nursery, given by Alice Bemis Taylor. At the southeast corner of Las Animas Street the Convention and Visitors Bureau operates in a colorful Victorian house.

About two miles south of downtown comes a multiple intersection. Stay in the center lane to continue south on Cascade across Cheyenne Boulevard. Reach Cheyenne Road and turn right. Note Lorraine and Fenmoor Streets to the right and just after Fenmoor turn left on Alsace Way. Follow Alsace as it turns right and then goes left up the hill. Pass Oak Avenue on the left and turn right at the next corner onto Polo Drive. This "back way" has brought you through Ivywild into the Broadmoor area, site of a world-class resort, tree-lined streets of elegant homes, and two fine small museums.

A Philadelphia blue-blood, Spencer Penrose, came to Colorado Springs in 1892 to partner his long-time friend, Charles Tutt, in a series of ventures. A first fortune came from Cripple Creek gold; then Penrose took a gamble on a new refining process. Used in conjunction with Utah copper mining, this made him a multi-millionaire. His financial reserves and his love of building backed a great case of "one-upmanship" — if anyone was going to do anything, Spec Penrose was going to do it better!

The Broadmoor area benefited from Penrose's largess through funds for the hotel complex and Cheyenne Mountain Zoo and Highway. Spec and other aristocratic young Easterners saw to the building of Cheyenne Mountain Country Club, one of the oldest in the nation, and brought polo to the Pikes Peak Region. A polo field stood left of Polo Drive until the 1960s.

Continue on Polo to a left turn onto Fourth, pass the Chapel of Our Savior and turn right onto Elm. Drive to First and turn right around the circle to reach the National Figure Skating Hall of Fame and Museum. Complete the circle to go south on First by Broadmoor's convention buildings, Colorado Hall and the International Center. Below the International Center, facing First, the Golden Bee welcomes visitors into a seventeenth-century English pub, fashioned from imported furnishings that languished for years in a New York warehouse.

The Broadmoor

Turn right on Lake Avenue and left on Lake Circle. To your left stands the small, circular Carriage House Museum, featuring pre-automobile vehicles and a custom-made Penrose Cadillac. To the right see the Broadmoor and Broadmoor South. All buildings in the complex except the golf club share the Mediterranean style with stucco walls and red tile roofs.

Although Spencer Penrose put Broadmoor on the map, his accomplishments built upon those of Count James Pourtales, who first gave prestige to the location. Count Pourtales envisioned deluxe homes occupying his Broadmoor City streets. His second continental style casino (fire destroyed the original) became the Broadmoor Golf Club.

To enjoy more Broadmoor homes, turn left just beyond the Carriage House on Beech Avenue and drive to Broadmoor Avenue. Continue to Hutton Lane, noting Colorado Springs School on the right. The main building, called the Trianon, copies Louis XIV's Versailles palace. Turn right on Hutton and right again on Pourtales Road to Mirada Road.

Turn left on Mirada and drive by two Broadmoor golf courses as you start up Cheyenne Mountain. Follow the signs to the zoo. Also on the mountain locate Will Rogers Shrine of the Sun and Ski Broadmoor.

Cheyenne Mountain Zoo reflects Spencer Penrose's desire to have a collection of western animals. Expanded to include world-wide species, the zoo on the mountain opened in 1936. Successful breeding of many rare and endangered animals ranks the facility among our nation's finest zoos.

Also attributable to the Broadmoor's builder, Will Rogers Shrine stands like an exclamation mark on the mountain above the zoo. The memorial, made of granite blocks cut from a single Cheyenne Mountain boulder, honors the beloved American humorist. Climb the tower to see three rooms of photographic memorabilia concerning Will Rogers and to look out over Colorado Springs. View the small chapel below the shrine where Mr. and Mrs. Penrose lie buried.

Ski Broadmoor opens its slopes to skiing in the winter and alpine sliding in the summer. The Winter House's deck makes a pleasant spot to observe either activity on the mountain.

Retrace your route to the intersection of Old Stage Road, Penrose Boulevard and Cheyenne Mountain Boulevard. Go straight ahead on Penrose to the stop sign and turn right to pass the World Arena and Broadmoor West. Turn left at Mesa Road to see Pauline Chapel, funded by Julie Penrose, and El Pomar, former estate of Mr. and Mrs. Penrose. Continue to the next intersection where you will see a sign for Seven Falls. Go straight ahead only one-tenth mile and turn right at a blind corner onto Evans. Drive downhill to Cheyenne Boulevard and find the entrances to South and North Cheyenne Canyons on your left.

The right road goes up North Cheyenne Canyon almost three miles to Helen Hunt Falls and the park Visitors Center. Continue uphill on the paved road until you can turn right onto Gold Camp Road, formerly the Short Line track to Cripple Creek. Drive carefully on the narrow road with its blind curves and take time to stop at the pulloffs. Pass through two old railroad tunnels and return to pavement in two and one-half miles. A pulloff shortly after the pavement resumes affords a panoramic view spanning the region from Garden of the Gods to Fort Carson.

In two miles take the right fork, Bear Creek Road, and reach Bear Creek Nature Center in less than one mile. A unit of the El Paso County Parks Department, Bear Creek Nature Center presents displays about local natural history in the building and a chance for first-hand observation on the network of short trails. Check out a Visitors Pack at the desk to enhance your exploring of the three natural habitats: creek bottom, mountain shrub and mountain meadow.

Turn right out of the Nature Center; resume your progress on Gold Camp Road by turning right at the next corner and drive to Twenty-first Street. Turn left and continue to Midland Expressway. To the right notice a single smokestack, the last remnant of four gold reduction mills that stood on the mesa. Trains traveling the Midland Railway from Cripple Creek brought ore to these mills for refining. The former Midland roundhouse on the left now houses Van Briggle Pottery.

(If you wish to return to town, turn right on Midland Expressway. If you wish to add on the West portion of the tour, continue straight ahead to Colorado Avenue. If you are beginning the West section from downtown, drive west on Colorado to Twenty-first.)

৫৯৩ WEST ৫৯৩

Proceed west on Colorado to reach Old Colorado City National Historic District. The first community in El Paso County, founded in 1859, now constitutes Colorado Springs' Old Town. Enjoy the shops, galleries and restaurants along Colorado Avenue.

Reach Thirtieth Street and turn right. Arrive at the road to Garden of the Gods in less than two miles and turn left. To your left find the entrance to White House Ranch, a living history museum where visitors step back in time to the nineteenth century. The costumed staff plays roles from different eras and expects you to join the fun. Meet the settler busy with his log cabin, smokehouse and small garden patch as he ponders possible Indian hostilities and welcomes other emigrants from the States. See how hands cared for stock and gardens on the working ranch and enjoy the general store in the old barn. Reconstruct the gracious life in Orchard House, built by General Palmer.

Return to the main road; turn left and enter Garden of the Gods, where the history of regional geology stands tall. A left turn within the park takes you toward the Visitors Center, but before reaching its parking lot, note the granite memorial on the left marking the Indian Trail.

Ute Indians from the western mountains and Plains Indians from the eastern prairies used the Indian Trail as a highway of their nomadic existence. This portion crossed the mesa to the east, skirted the Garden of the Gods, passed Manitou's springs, and provided access to and from the mountains via Ute Pass.

After stopping at the Visitors Center to view displays detailing the history, geology and ecology of the park, turn left out of the parking lot and drive to the first intersection. Turn left to visit the Garden's High Point, viewing Cheyenne Mountain to the south and Pikes Peak to the west.

Return to the intersection and bear left. You will be winding back and forth within Garden of the Gods with plenty of opportunities to view the rock formations, take pictures, enjoy a short hike, or have a picnic. Drive about one mile to the stop sign; turn left and continue on the main

19

Three Graces — Garden of the Gods

road, Garden Drive, through the park to Balanced Rock and Steamboat Rock. You may stop in the parking lot before the two rocks or drive between them and turn left to circle the other side of Steamboat Rock.

Return on Garden Drive to Hidden Inn. Drive between the Gateway Rocks and turn left on a one-way road by the park's eastern boundary. Note the geologic information signs. After swinging around the curve and driving partway down the hill, you will find a pulloff on the left. Proceed to the stop sign, turn left, pass Hidden Inn once more, and exit the park. Drive back to Thirtieth and turn left to the first intersection.

To visit Glen Eyrie Castle continue straight ahead to the first left turn and bear left down the hill. (Remember to phone The Navigators for tour and drive-through hours.) General Palmer first built here in Queen's Canyon in 1871. Later he constructed the 67-room stone castle, complete with electric lights, telephone, weather system, and all the necessities and amenities to make the estate self-contained. The property now belongs to The Navigators, an international, nondenominational Christian group.

The tour turns sharp right to ascend the road that crosses the Mesa back toward downtown. At the top of the hill find an overlook, a perfect place to bid farewell to our tour of Colorado Springs.

Continue east, passing the private Garden of the Gods Club and Kissing Camels Golf Club. Drive to the end of Mesa Road, turn left on Uintah, and reach Interstate 25 to return to downtown.

FOOTHILLS
THREE TRIPS ON WHEELS NORTH

This section leads one along the foothills from Colorado Springs to Denver. Explore the United States Air Force Academy. Visit the Tri-Lakes area of Monument, Palmer Lake and Woodmoor. Enjoy a day in Colorado's state capital. All three tours offer attractions that remain available year around. Only rarely does Interstate 25 between Colorado Springs and Denver close because of snow, although Monument Hill can be as troublesome as a mountain pass in bad weather. Colorado's Eastern Slope receives only one-fourth the snow that the Western Slope does; you will find many beautiful days for adventuring at any time of year.

These three destinations line up along Interstate 25 north of Colorado Springs. You may wish to take two days and begin with the Air Force Academy and Tri-Lakes. Continue to Denver for an overnight stay; spend the next day enjoying the Mile High City and return to Colorado Springs.

UNITED STATES
AIR FORCE ACADEMY

The world-famous Air Force Academy Chapel draws more visitors than any other man-made Colorado attraction. The public is welcome to attend regular worship services and musical programs. There are, however, times when special services, such as wedding ceremonies, close at least a portion of the building. Try to check with the Visitors Center first to avoid disappointments.

Check also for special events such as a band concert or a planetarium show. If you plan to attend a presentation at the planetarium, arrive on time; doors close promptly and latecomers will not be admitted.

If you tour the Academy during the academic year, be in the Chapel area by noon on weekdays to see the Cadet Wing's luncheon formation.

You can extend the north portion of the Colorado Springs tour to include the Academy by turning north on I-25 from Uintah Street, or add USAFA to the end of the Tri-Lakes trip.

Mileage: 45 miles　　　　　　　　　　　　　　　　*Actual driving time: 1 hour*

Plans for USAFA began moving forward after President Eisenhower signed a congressional bill authorizing the newest service academy in April 1954. The Secretary of the Air Force appointed a Site Selection Committee, including Charles Lindbergh. Supporters proposed 582 different locations in forty-five states, and the committee covered 21,000 miles inspecting possible sites. Colorado Springs emerged as the winner among three finalists.

In July 1955 interim facilities at Lowry Air Force Base in Denver welcomed the first class of cadets and construction at the permanent site began. Academy personnel relocated in their new home to begin fall classes in 1958 and to graduate the initial class of 207 in June 1959. Congress authorized the inclusion of women students at all service schools in 1976.

Approximately 1,500 new fourth class students, called "doolies," gain admission to the Academy each year. Members of Congress nominate the majority. The number of women students matches the ratio that exists between men and women in the Air Force, about twelve percent. Also echoing Air Force organization, four groups divided into forty squadrons compose the Cadet Wing, authorized to number 4,500. Each squadron contains members of all four classes, with seniors serving as cadet officers and juniors and sophomores as non-commissioned officers.

Academic classes usually contain less than twenty students. During their first two years, cadets concentrate on a core curriculum designed to broaden and diversify their knowledge. Upperclass students select from some twenty academic majors, implemented by core classes. Including military training and physical education, cadets amass between 180 and 186 semester hours before graduating as commissioned officers with a Bachelor of Science degree.

Cadets understand the school's assumption that their behavior will reflect the principles of honor and professional ethics. All classes acknowledge the Cadet Honor Code: "We will not lie, steal or cheat nor tolerate among us those who do. Furthermore, I resolve to do my duty to live honorably, so help me God."

USAFA publicity notes that the mission of the school is "to provide instruction and experience to all cadets so that they graduate with the knowledge and character essential to leadership and the motivation to become career officers in the United States Air Force." The Academy's theme is "Commitment to Excellence"; cadets, faculty and staff share in this purpose and dedication.

To engender these ideals, cadets receive rigorous training from the time they enter as doolies. New fourth class students immediately undergo six weeks of Basic Cadet Training, including field experience, designed to increase their self-confidence to face Academy challenges. Third class cadets learn to meet land and water aircrew emergencies in a program of survival, evasion, resistance, and escape (SERE). Upperclass students must spend three summer weeks on duty at an Air Force base.

Covering 18,000 acres and backdropped by the Rampart Range of the Rockies, the Academy straddles five mesas and spills over into the valleys between them. The Chicago architectural firm of Skidmore, Owings and Merrill implemented its contemporary designs in glass, aluminum, steel, marble, and granite. Cost of the land totaled $4.2 million and of the buildings, $221 million.

Begin this tour by driving north from Colorado Springs on Interstate 25. You may take Exit 147 to visit Prorodeo Hall of Champions and Museum of the American Cowboy, national headquarters of the Prorodeo Cowboys Association.

Rodeo has blossomed into a popular sport since the days when saddle-bred cowboys let off steam in competitive contests designed to show their ability with horses and cattle. Those men spent weeks in the saddle, through hundreds of miles of harsh and dangerous country, conveying beef on the hoof to western railheads for shipment east to processors and markets. Popular belief has it that the first publicly-attended rodeo took place on July 4, 1869, at Deer Trail, Colorado. Colorado Springs' annual Pikes Peak or Bust celebration rates among the nation's top rodeos.

Leave the Interstate at the South Entrance to the Air Force Academy (Exit 150B). Ask the guard at the gate for a visitors guide, and plan to stop at the Visitors Center for information.

Enter USAFA on South Gate Boulevard. Continue to the Airmanship Overlook and turn right into the parking lot. A T-38 Talon aircraft, appearing ready to soar, pays tribute to the Thunderbirds, the Air Force precision flying team. From the overlook view the Academy airstrip, site of light plane, sailplane and parachute activities of the cadet airmanship program. Single engine, white and red T-41 planes serve as cadet trainers. Watch for the tandem performance of yellow tow planes leading sailplanes into position to catch the natural air currents.

Proceed on South Gate Boulevard to Stadium Drive and turn right to reach Falcon Stadium. Business and civic leaders created the Air Force Academy Foundation and spearheaded a fund-raising drive to finance the stadium. Civilians and members of the Air Force donated $3.5 million to provide all the necessary construction money. Temporary bleachers can stretch the stadium's seating capacity to 50,000 for football games and graduation exercises.

Air Force teams take their name from the school's mascot. An Arctic gyrfalcon reigns as the official mascot, but native Colorado prairie falcons perform at football halftimes. To train and fly the birds cadets in the falconry club must pass the Colorado Raptors Exam for anyone working with captive birds of prey (raptors). An Air Force officer, a veterinarian, supervises the program and the falcons' home, called the mews.

Pass Falcon Stadium and turn left on Academy Drive. Proceeding west you will catch glimpses on the right of the 36-hole Eisenhower Golf Course. Next on your right will be the Officers' Club and after crossing Interior Drive view the hospital on the left.

Beyond the hospital follow Academy Drive as it swings right. USAFA acreage constitutes a national wildlife preserve, and you may see mule deer grazing peacefully on the grounds. Stop at the Nature Trail Overlook. The very short trail's end provides a head-on view of the Chapel framed by ponderosa pines.

Continue on Academy Drive to Falcon Sign 5 and turn right to the Cadet Area. Observe instructions for visitors parking near the planetarium. Buildings in the Cadet Area open to the public, with certain limitations, include the planetarium, Arnold Hall, the Chapel, and the library. The planetarium staff instructs cadets in astronautics, astronomy and celestial navigation. Public presentations occur daily in the summer and on weekends during the rest of the year.

Arnold Hall, the cadets' social center, opens portions of its ground level to visitors. Cadet social activities center on this building. In the lobby view display cases with Air Force memorabilia and go up the few stairs to see the theater. Turn left from the lobby to view the winding staircase that descends to the ballroom.

Leave Arnold Hall. Go up the stairs and pass Harmon Hall, the administration building. Walk east to view the quadrangle. Cadets live in two dormitories: Vandenburg Hall stands east of Arnold; Sijan Hall, south of the Chapel. Fairchild Hall, at a right angle to Vandenburg across the east side of the complex, contains classrooms, laboratories and the library. The Academy library features a central staircase spiraling up its four levels and on the top floor the Gimbel Aeronautical Library, detailing the history of man's desire to fly. Mitchell Hall, between Sijan and the south end of Fairchild, provides dining space for the full cadet wing.

Dominating the Cadet Area the multi-denominational Chapel thrusts its seventeen spires skyward. The building contains a Protestant chapel on its upper level with Catholic and Jewish chapels and an all-faith meeting room below. Although $3.5 million in government funds built the Chapel, the interior furnishings came completely from private donations.

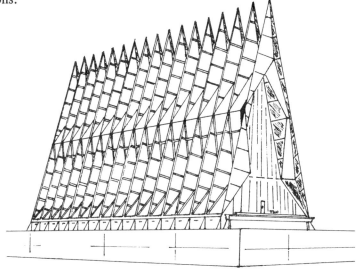

From the 99-foot height of its tetrahedrons to the heavily sound-proofed floor, from the majestic 4,334-pipe organ at the rear to the "Soaring Spirit" Cross above the altar, the interdenominational Protestant Chapel provides an awesome place of worship. More than 24,000 pieces of stained glass separate the spires. Colorado semi-precious stones created the reredos behind the altar, and white Italian marble forms the altar and pulpit. The chapel accommodates 1,200 people.

Before entering the Catholic Chapel, you will find a written and pictorial display concerning work on, and a computer-created cast of, the Shroud of Turin. Academy personnel have played a large role in the investigation.

The 500-seat Our Lady of the Skies Chapel features marble bas-reliefs of Mary, the Holy Spirit Dove and the Guardian Angel set against the mosaic altar screen, an abstract rendering of the elements of Creation. Each Station of the Cross includes a small cross made from olivewood obtained at the Mount of Olives.

Jerusalem brownstone blocks pave the Jewish Chapel's foyer. Translucent walls of the circular chapel reveal colorful stained glass sides of the surrounding square. The chapel focuses on the Holy Ark, repository of two handwritten, ramskin scrolls of the Torah. Beginning letters of the Ten Commandments appear in Hebrew on the front of the Ark. The three-dimensional Star of David on the right centers the Eternal Light; the seven-branched Menorah appears to the left.

Crowning the hill west of the Chapel stands a memorial tower. The American Legion dedicated this monument to the Cadet Wing in honor of all who have served their country. East of the Chapel lies the center courtyard of the Cadet Area where displays include planes, bronze busts of Wilbur and Orville Wright and "The Fledgings" statue of a mother eagle with her young. The latter carries the inscription, "Man's flight through life is sustained by the power of his knowledge."

Leave the Cadet Area, return to Academy Drive and turn right. Note playing fields on your right and after the road turns east stop at the first overlook to view the entire athletic complex.

Cadets must take physical education classes each year and be able to swim. The intercollegiate program features everything from football to fencing, from wrestling to water polo. All cadets not in varsity sports must join their squadrons' teams in intramurals.

The cadet gymnasium on the right includes two pools, a pistol and rifle range and facilities for volleyball, boxing, wrestling, squash, handball, fencing, and gymnastics. Thirty-three tennis courts front the building, and 125 acres accommodate outdoor sports including soccer and lacrosse. You may not view the gym but the Field House welcomes visitors. Continue east on Academy Drive to Field House Drive and turn right. As you enter the building, you will see an ice arena to your right and the basketball stadium to the left. Straight ahead, on each side of the gift shop, look through the windows to view the multi-purpose track and football facility.

Return on Field House Drive to North Gate Boulevard and turn right. At the corner of Stadium Boulevard, look right to see the B-52 bomber, "Diamond Lil." The Strategic Air Command used these 185,000-pound bombers for some thirty years. In 1984 an Air Force crew flew "Lil" to Peterson Air Force Base, and trucks brought her twenty miles to the present installation.

Leaving USAFA, drive to the north gate and cross Interstate 25 to visit the Western Museum of Mining and Industry, located behind the 1890s red and white farmhouse. Enjoy informative displays on everything from placer mining in streams to hardrock efforts underground. Follow the handling of ore from assay office to refining mill. Working machinery and do-it-yourself gold panning provide treats at the museum and an excellent background for future Trips on Wheels to old mining towns.

Return to I-25 and turn south to reach Colorado Springs.

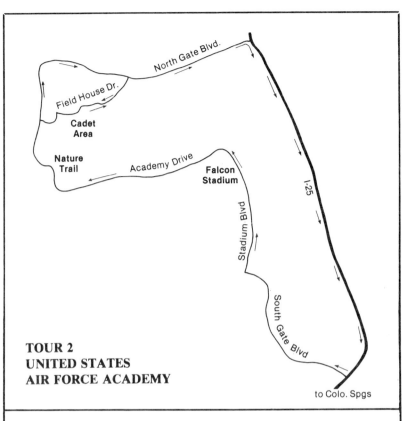

**TOUR 2
UNITED STATES
AIR FORCE ACADEMY**

North Gate Blvd.

Field House Dr.

Cadet Area

Nature Trail

Academy Drive

Falcon Stadium

Stadium Blvd

I-25

South Gate Blvd

to Colo. Spgs

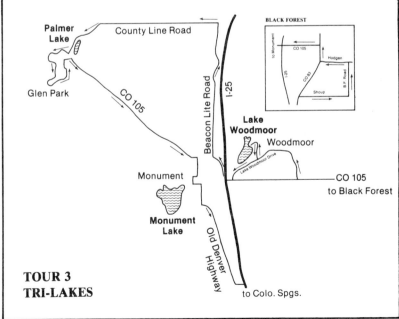

**TOUR 3
TRI-LAKES**

Palmer Lake

County Line Road

Glen Park

CO 105

Beacon Lite Road

I-25

Monument

Monument Lake

Old Denver Highway

Lake Woodmoor

Woodmoor

Lake Woodmoor Drive

CO 105
to Black Forest

to Colo. Spgs.

BLACK FOREST

to Monument

CO 105

Hodgen

I-25

CO 83

B.F. Road

Shoup

TRI-LAKES: MONUMENT, PALMER LAKE, WOODMOOR

Move from forest to prairie to lake to foothills and from wide open country to settled community in this tour of contrasts and opposites.

North of the Mine Shopping Center on Woodmoor Drive locate Wildlife World Museum. With some 5,000 pieces, the museum has the largest collection of wildlife fine art in the world.

In the small town of Larkspur the Colorado Renaissance Festival holds forth on weekends during June and the first half of July. Begun in 1977, the festival features crafts, entertainment, food, clothing, and buildings in the Renaissance theme. Go north on I-25 to Exit 173 and follow the signs west.

Locate the National Carvers Museum at tour's end by crossing Baptist Road and following the signs for less than one mile. See examples of the woodcarvers' art for whittlers in fact or at heart.

Mileage: 55 miles   *Actual driving time: 1½ hours*

Mention "the Divide" in Colorado and most people think of the Continental Divide, separating waters in their flow east and west. A second, north-south divide juts out from the mountains between Colorado Springs and Denver, channeling waters north to the Platte River and south to the Arkansas. The local Arkansas or Palmer Divide area includes the Tri-Lakes communities of Monument, Palmer Lake and Woodmoor. Larkspur lies to the north and Black Forest to the east.

Monument Station, four miles south of the Divide's summit, occupied a site close to the "Dirty Woman's Ranche" of 1860. An old woman living along Monument Creek shared her dwelling with pigs. Early soldiers and travelers reported not wanting to eat at her home because of the filth.

Named for Monument Rock, containing Monument Lake and split by Monument Creek, Monument's settlement predated Colorado Springs' founding and the coming of railroads. This Upper Monument Valley location attracted both farmers and ranchers and contains the oldest home in the region, the 1860s McShane House. A tunnel formerly linked the homestead to a small Old Stone Fort, defense for settlers against marauding Arapaho and Cheyenne Indians.

Monument typified the diverse economy of the Divide locale, while Palmer Lake reflected its vacation lure. In Monument large scale lumbering operations provided ties for the developing railroads and much of the building material for eastern Colorado and northern New Mexico. Farmers found the district ideal for raising bumper crops of potatoes. Herdsmen, too, found the fertile, well-watered elevation a paradise. Milk from dairy farms went to a cheese factory in Larkspur. In Monument a creamery and an ice house existed side by side. Blocks of ice cut from both Monument and Palmer Lakes preserved produce on Denver and Rio Grande trains. In contrast to the industrious community of Monument, Palmer Lake developed as a health and pleasure resort. Picnickers arrived from Denver to enjoy the scenic beauty. An early reference christens it "The Gem of the Rockies" and sings its praises: "The Great Artist has penciled in. . .peaks and cliffs; sunlight glen. . .flowery vale. . .gaping caverns. . .pillared palisades."

Dr. W. Finley Thompson promoted the development of Palmer Lake. Dr. Thompson, born and educated in New York and practicing dentistry in San Francisco, injured his head in a diving accident and went to Europe to recover. He became a society dentist in London and amassed a net worth of $60,000 in five years. With his grubstake and a speculator's enthusiasm, Dr. Thompson visualized the site of Palmer Lake as the Interlaken of America, founded the town of Palmer Lake and became its first mayor.

The year of 1887 found Dr. Thompson busy building his estate, Estemere, and the Chautauqua Assembly putting down roots. Estemere, a delightful enclave of Victoriana in the Rockies, featured everything from a billiard room to an observatory. Unfortunately Dr. Thompson found himself overextended, left the country under a cloud and died in Mexico in 1892.

The Chautauqua Movement held its first assembly in New York State in 1874, promoting the idea of combining one's summer vacation in an idyllic setting with educational pursuits. The Palmer Lake Chautauqua headquartered at Glen Park, providing Assembly grounds for Colorado, Arizona and Wyoming. Sunlit glens and flowery vales witnessed such "social and intellectual treats" as field and nature walks, excursions, recitals, concerts, dramatic entertainments, lectures, and Bible classes. For example, the 1890-91 Chautauqua course spotlighted English literature in eight chapters from Chaucer to Tennyson. In 1891-92 the Movement surveyed "Social Institutions of the United States," including bar, bench, railroads, Wall Street, universities, and churches.

To accommodate visitors arriving on twenty-eight daily trains from Denver, Rockland Hotel, "the most accessible summer resort in Colorado," opened in 1889. At the turn of the century one could enjoy a day's stay at the Rockland for two or three dollars. However, a far greater bargain existed at the Chautauqua in Glen Park where eleven dollars a month provided a 10 x 12-foot tent (with floor).

The coming of the automobile spelled a decline in railroad travel. The Chautauqua ceased assembling after its 1910 season. Fire destroyed the Rockland in 1920. But the lure of pillared palisades and pleasures of small town living continue to make Palmer Lake a popular year-around location.

Begin this tour at the intersection of Interstate 25 and Academy Boulevard, opposite the south entrance to the Air Force Academy and nine miles north of downtown Colorado Springs. Leave I-25 at Exit 150A and be prepared to turn left immediately at the first stoplight onto Colorado Highway 83.

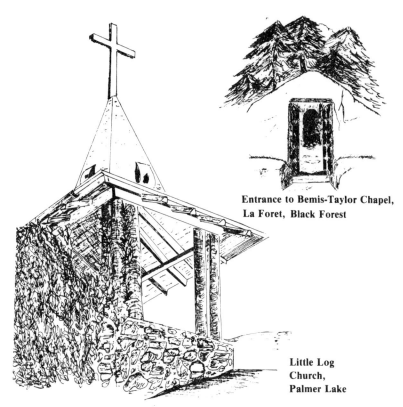

Entrance to Bemis-Taylor Chapel,
La Foret, Black Forest

Little Log
Church,
Palmer Lake

Proceed north on Highway 83 for five miles. Turn right on Shoup Road and after two miles start watching the street signs to spot Peregrine Way on your left. Prepare to turn left in another two-tenths of a mile at Milam Road to Black Forest Regional Park.

The 1971 formation of the El Paso Park and Recreation District recognized the need to preserve open space and to relieve the heavy use of Colorado Springs parks. In 1978 the county acquired a 25-year lease to 240 acres and began Black Forest Park. The facility includes playing fields, tennis courts and a trail loop for hikers and cross country skiers. Much of the acreage remains in its natural state, nestled in the ponderosa pine forest, and offers majestic mountain views. It deserves a stop for a picnic, a walk or just a quick beauty break.

Return to Shoup Road and turn left. In one-half mile look for the La Foret sign on the right. This acreage contains the former summer home of Alice Bemis Taylor, donor of the Colorado Springs Fine Arts Center. She bequeathed the La Foret property for use as a Christian camp and conference grounds. In addition to the present Ponderosa Lodge Mrs. Taylor built a striking private chapel in memory of her husband. Reminiscent of Southwest mission style it features stark white stucco walls, decorative wood carving and an altar screen by artist Eugenie Shonnard.

Continue on Shoup Road to the traffic light and turn left on Black Forest Road. This intersection marks the heart of the Black Forest community.

Cheyenne and Arapaho Indians treasured Black Forest's 150,000 acres of ponderosa pines as an ideal campsite providing water, good hunting and material for shelter and fuel. White settlers arrived in the 1860s. Later General Palmer purchased 45,000 acres for his Colorado Pinery and Land Company. Loggers chopped trees; sawmills cut ties for the railroads and boards for Colorado Springs buildings. Subsequently, lumbering became a major Black Forest industry, with some forty-five sawmills operating before World War I.

Proceed north on Black Forest Road four miles until you must turn onto Hodgen. Go left, following the signs to Monument, and proceed west three and one-half miles to a right turn at Highway 83. Another two miles north brings you to Colorado Highway 105 and a left turn to head west once more. This region preserves many examples of the ranching and farming heritage, both abandoned and operating: farmhouses, barns, windmills, barbed wire fences.

Drive west four miles on Highway 105. Pass Winding Meadow Way and Briarhaven Court; turn right on Lake Woodmoor Drive for one mile to Lower Lake Drive. Turn right again to skirt the east edge of Lake Woodmoor, first of the three small lakes that give the Tri-Lakes region its name. Follow Lower Lake one-half mile to a deadend, turn around, retrace your route back to Lake Woodmoor Drive, and turn right. In one-half mile, at Woodmoor Drive, the main tour turns left to Highway 105; however, you may turn right to reach Wildlife World Museum.

To visit Palmer Lake, follow Highway 105 across the Interstate for one-half mile and turn right onto Beacon Lite. Look to the right to see Monument's cemetery, site of some pioneer graves and excellent examples of the Hassell iron fences made in Colorado City.

Beacon Lite continues two miles north to County Line Road, the boundary between El Paso and Douglas Counties. Turn left on County Line and head back toward the mountains and the town of Palmer Lake two and one-half miles west. Just before County Line meets Highway 105 you will be crossing multiple railroad tracks that brought both the Denver and Rio Grande and the Atchison, Topeka and Santa Fe into town. South of this crossing the two railroads coexisted on opposite shores, sandwiching the lake between them. The D&RG kept to the west; the Santa Fe held the east bank. In a welcome metamorphosis, the former AT&SF right-of-way becomes El Paso County Park's New Santa Fe Trail with Palmer Lake as a recreational area and trailhead.

Turn left on Highway 105 to visit the town of Palmer Lake, noting the lake on the left. Lake and land both bear the name of Colorado Springs' founder, General William Jackson Palmer. *(Be aware that in spite of all the turns and the many roads involved, driving distance within Palmer Lake and Glen Park totals only three and one-half miles!)*

Less than one-half mile from your turn onto Highway 105, note the sign for the Little Log Church and turn right on Pie Corner, then left on Upper Glenway. Just before the stop sign find the church on the right. Many engaged couples pick as their wedding place the small non-denominational church, founded in 1925.

Continue past the stop sign and straight ahead uphill on Thompson to Hillside and turn left. On your right stands the Vaile Hill Art Gallery, bearing the name of Palmer Lake's benefactress, Lucretia Vaile. The Vaile family, headed by Lucretia's father, attorney for the D&RG, lived in Denver and maintained a summer home in Palmer Lake. Miss Vaile moved away but returned to live in this modest house, later willing to the town her home and funds that helped build the local library and museum.

Continue on Hillside for a view to the left of Dr. Thompson's Estemere estate. The yellow, clapboard-sided, red-roofed mansion features the usual Victorian conglomeration of gables, turrets and fancy woodwork. The grounds contain a small chapel and a gazebo with an ornamental iron fence patrolling the massive stone retaining wall. Still a private residence, Estemere and its grounds are not open to the public.

Turn left on South Valley, passing old cottages on the right and following Estemere property on the left. At the corner of Glenway look left to see the gazebo. Continue a short distance on South Valley, viewing two historic buildings on the right: McIntyre House and Pillsbury Store. Pass these two structures and turn right on Old Carriage Road to reach Glen Park.

Site of the former Chautauqua Assembly, Glen Park boasts over ninety quaint cottages from Chautauqua days, some abandoned but many now private homes. Within Glen Park you face frequent turns, slow speed and narrow, sometimes steep dirt roads, but also a unique location, a great topside view and a short distance. Go right on Walnut, right again on Crescent, pass Largo, and go right at the next street, Bonita. Follow Bonita uphill two blocks until it swings left and becomes Verano. When you reach the highest point, by the roof of a square cottage with a wrap-around porch, stop and view the eastern plains, Black Forest, the northern reaches of Colorado Springs, and the rock formation called Elephant Rock. The elephant's trunk stands away from the body separated by a narrow arch.

Continue to the end of Verano, make one hairpin turn left and start back downhill on Largo. Remember the distances are very short. Turn right on Bonita, left on Corona, right on Chautauqua, and left on Corso. At the stop sign turn left on Virginia; at the sign for Walnut continue downhill and turn left on the first road. You will pass Glen Park, another unit of the El Paso County Parks department, on your left.

If you do not want to bother with the up and downhill roller coaster of Glen Park, a short loop at the bottom gives you an idea of the cottages and the Assembly site. To stay below do not turn right on Crescent but continue straight ahead on the narrow pavement to the stop sign. Turn left on Virginia and left again by the park.

Continue to the stop sign and turn right on Valley Crescent to exit Glen Park. Cross South Valley Road, continue to the next stop sign at Lower Glenway and immediately across the intersection turn right into the parking lot. Here you will find the Lucretia Vaile Library-Museum. The excellent small museum, dating from 1982, traces Palmer Lake's history. The exterior, complete with a gazebo to the building's left, conforms to traditional architecture.

Across the street spot Palmer Lake's Town Hall and the Yule Log sign. Each December Palmer Lake continues a tradition of hunting the hidden yule log begun in 1934. The finder wins a ride back to town on the log to join the community celebration.

To leave Palmer Lake, continue to the end of the block; turn right on Middle Glenway and right again on Highway 105 toward Monument. On this three-mile stretch of road spot Camp Elephant Rock on the right and Elephant Rock itself off to the left.

As you near Monument, you will see a sign on the left saying "Pioneer Lookout" and ahead the D&RG overpass above the highway. Between these two points, on the right, is a small stone marker commemorating the site of the Old Stone Fort. Beyond the marker stands the McShane House, its protective walls built two to three feet thick. Please respect this private property.

Drive under the D&RG tracks and turn right on Washington into the town of Monument. The community advertises its altitude as 6,800 feet and its incorporation date as 1879 and claims its citizens remain "Proud of our past — confident of our future."

In contrast to Palmer Lake, Monument's streets feature the classic grid pattern. Drive on Washington to the stop sign at Third and turn right. Turn left on Front and left again on Second, noting Limbach Park on the right. As Monument experiences a building boom, many of the historic structures vanish, but keep your eyes open for survivors.

Turn right on Jefferson. Between Second and First spot a 1911 church, typical of the small frame churches of early settlements. Across the street, Inez Johnson Lewis School honors a former El Paso County superintendent of schools who became state superintendent.

Follow Jefferson out of town until you must turn left and then right on Old Denver Road. Continue two miles more to Baptist Road. Across the road, see the signs to the National Carvers Museum. Take Baptist Road east to I-25 and drive south to Colorado Springs.

Two routes through Denver join a number of attractions. Leetsdale Drive and Speer Boulevard take you on a southeast to northwest diagonal course stretching from Four Mile House Historic Park to Elitch Gardens. City Park to the north and Washington Park to the south bracket a roughly north-south excursion to parks and homes. Each route covers approximately eight miles and requires about twenty minutes to drive. You can easily select points of interest from both itineraries.

In addition to the two detailed routes, a separate section on downtown spotlights places you can visit from either tour. If you do not mind walking a few blocks, you may enjoy this district more by leaving your car at a long-term parking lot close to either Larimer Square or the Capitol and taking advantage of the shuttle on Sixteenth Street.

For a full program of Denver's offerings visit the Convention and Visitors Bureau in the small triangle bounded by West Colfax, Court and Fourteenth.

Mileage: 135-150 miles   Actual driving time: 3-3½ hours

"Pikes Peak or Bust!" chorused the Fifty-niners. In 1858 discovery of a small deposit of gold near the confluence of Cherry Creek and the South Platte River sparked a swelling tide of argonauts heading for the Rockies. Pikes Peak never was involved, and many went bust. However, the "gold in them thar hills" led to an 1859 invasion as miners struck paydirt at Black Hawk, Central City and Idaho Springs. Gold and silver occasioned the founding of many Colorado cities, and Denver tops the list.

Cherry Creek bisected two infant communities in 1858. Auraria held forth on the west side while St. Charles occupied land to the east. A change of ownership brought a change in name, and St. Charles became Denver City in honor of the Kansas Territorial Governor, General James W. Denver. Auraria and Denver City merged in 1860 to become Denver, the major supply center for mountain mining camps.

The 1860 election of Abraham Lincoln sent southern congressmen home from Washington, clearing the way to create Colorado Territory on February 28, 1861. Colorado City and Golden each took turns as territorial capital, but Denver's selection put an end to the government's nomadic ways.

To the west gold still reigned as king, thanks to a new smelting process in the mid-1870s that permitted local ore reduction. The seventies also saw a new royal metal challenger; the silver era began and Colorado acquired a nickname, the Silver State. Statehood came in 1876 heralding another name, the Centennial State.

With all the wealth pouring into Denver from the mountains, transportation became the major concern. Transcontinental railroad plans placed tracks across Wyoming where Continental Divide passes scaled much lower elevations. A slump hit Denver as people feared the Colorado capital would lose its "Queen City of the Plains" designation to Cheyenne. The construction of Denver Pacific track from Cheyenne to Denver averted panic, and the Kansas Pacific Railroad rushed to finish its line from the east, laying more than ten miles of track in ten hours. Solving the transportation problem encouraged an influx of people and commerce. Denver's population topped 106,000 in 1890, a year in which Colorado Springs numbered only 11,000.

Although silver collapsed with the worldwide 1893 economic crash, Colorado's earth continued to yield its treasures. Denver shared with Colorado Springs in the Cripple Creek bonanza. World War I began a new mining story with molybdenum and vanadium, both used in steel manufacturing, and uranium. Oil and natural gas presaged an energy boom.

Rails served both trade and travelers. Automobiles brought even more visitors and, ironically, a playback of the old transportation problems. Building mountain roads proved to be as difficult and costly as building mountain railroads.

World War II had a profound effect on Colorado's future. Not only did scientific, research and military installations locate here, but also many armed services personnel remembered their former duty station with pleasure and returned after the war.

Once the country's largest silver producer, Colorado became the free world's greatest molybdenum source. A uranium rush yielded $133 million in ore. Tourism continued to burgeon and Denver, always in the middle of Colorado happenings, developed into an international city.

A variety of people, products and happenings continue to enliven the bustling city of both mountains and plains. Denver has been home for writers Eugene Field, Gene Fowler and Damon Runyon; Antoinette Perry, for whom Broadway's Tony awards are named; Mamie Eisenhower, and former Miss America, Marilyn VanDerbur. Singer John Denver appropriated the city's name. Samsonite luggage and Russell Stover candies began in the Mile High City. Avid football fans cheer the Denver Broncos. The state capital continues to provide a central hub of government, finance, business, and transportation to ranchers and farmers, energy explorations and manufacturing, scientific research and educational institutions.

Begin this tour on Colorado Highway 83 and drive north forty-three miles from Colorado Springs to the town of Parker. The settlement grew up twenty miles south of Denver as the final stage stop before the city. James S. Parker served as proprietor of the 1864 Twenty Mile House: first house in Parker, refuge from Indian attacks and a welcome stopover for early emigrants and travelers. The Smoky Hill Trail from the east to the goldfields passed this way as did both the Smoky Hill and the Santa Fe, Butterfield and Wells Fargo stage lines.

Between Parker and the Denver suburb of Aurora, find greenhouses

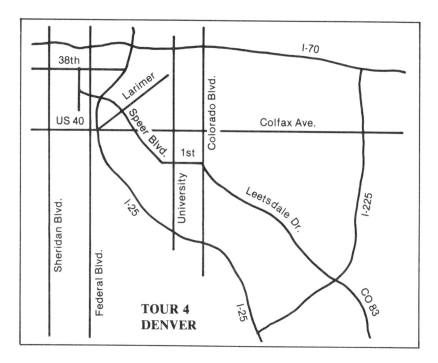

on the left. Growers raise both roses and Colorado's famed carnations for wholesale distribution.

When you reach Denver, Parker Road become Leetsdale Drive; watch for the continuing Colorado 83 signs. In two miles turn left at Forest Street and follow the signs to Four Mile Historic Park.

ᥱ᥊᥍᥆ ROUTE 1 ᥱ᥊᥍᥆

Built in 1859, Four Mile House is Denver's oldest structure. Until the 1870 completion of the railroad, Four Mile House, a tavern and wayside inn four miles from Denver, welcomed new arrivals. The park includes a stagecoach stop and experiences of life on prairie, ranch and farm. Indian tipi, Broadmoor stagecoach, a collection of buildings, and a variety of outdoor areas offer an experience analogous to White House Ranch in Colorado Springs.

Return to Leetsdale via Cherry Street, turn left and get into the right lane to continue on 83 to Colorado Boulevard. Turn right on Colorado and be prepared to turn left immediately at the traffic light on First Avenue. Follow First less than two miles past Cherry Creek Shopping Center and the Denver Country Club until it leads to Speer Boulevard's diagonal route toward downtown Denver. Cross Broadway; pass the Denver Center for the Performing Arts on the right and Auraria Higher Education Center on the left. Turn right on Lawrence Street; turn left on Eighteenth Street and left again on Larimer to reach Larimer Square.

36

William Larimer, Denver City's founder, came to the Rockies from Pennsylvania by way of Nebraska and Kansas. Caught up in the Pikes Peak or Bust craze, Larimer came equipped with the experience and nerve of a born promoter. The founders of St. Charles had staked claim to a townsite on Cherry Creek only two weeks before but failed to obtain official recognition. In a case of urban claim jumping, supposedly either through plying with liquor the one man left to guard the property or by suggesting to him the finality of hanging, Larimer moved in and organized the Denver City Company. At a time when Colfax and Broadway represented the city limits, Larimer Street became a center of the infant city's business, culture and politics.

Late nineteenth century Victorian structures held on through skid row days until a revival loomed with the organization of the Larimer Square enterprise in 1964. The fine old brick buildings emerged from a good cleaning with forgotten architectural details intact and visible, and in 1971 Larimer's 1400 block became Denver's first Landmark Preservation District. The successful efforts of Larimer Square's believers helped spark many of the new developments in lower downtown. Explore Larimer Square's distinctive shops and restaurants along the street and tucked away in arcades and around corners.

Larimer Square approximates the location of short-lived St. Charles and early Denver City; the Auraria campus across Cherry Creek echoes the site of Auraria town. In 1860 representatives met on a bridge spanning the creek to consolidate the two communities into Denver.

Auraria Higher Education Complex features a 169-acre campus encompassing three separate schools: Community College, Metro State and University of Colorado at Denver. It makes a pleasant stroll to walk across the Larimer Street Bridge to the campus, where several historic buildings help you imagine the way it was.

The Tivoli Building on the right began life as the Tivoli Union Brewery in 1860 and ceased operations in 1969. The old brewery now houses a shopping, theater and restaurant complex. One block left see the tiny Emmanuel-Sherith Israel Chapel (1876) and St. Cajetan's Church. Both buildings yield to new interior use but preserve their exteriors.

Continue past the front of St. Cajetan's to Ninth Street Historic Park, Denver's oldest residential block. Thirteen houses, some from territorial days, and one old store create a peaceful oasis in the bustling campus. Plantings, iron fences, original granite curbing, and flagstone sidewalks reinforce the authenticity of restored Victorian homes.

Also on campus find St. Elizabeth's, built in 1896, and still functioning as a parish church. Adjacent to St. Elizabeth's stands a memorial to Frederick G. Bonfils. Fred Bonfils partnered ownership of the *Denver Post* with Harry Tammen. Bonfils and Tammen alternated publicity stunts and yellow journalism with crusading zeal and community service.

Continue west on Speer Boulevard from the Larimer Square-Auraria district. In the early 1970s parks and modern buildings began replacing urban eyesores along Speer. One more striking development involved reviving the South Platte River from a garbage flow into the Platte River Greenway. Streaming past a series of parks with picnic areas, hiking and bike paths, the cleansed waterway also offers boating and fishing. Follow Speer until it ends, turn right on Irving and left on Thirty-eighth; drive less than one mile more to Elitch Gardens.

Ninth Street Historic Park

John Elitch ran a restaurant on Larimer Street, supplying his own produce from an orchard and truck garden northwest of the city. In 1890 he decided to convert the farm into an amusement park that included Denver's first zoo, a summer stock theater, band concerts, and a daring balloonist-aerialist, all set against a background of elaborate flower gardens. An immediate success, Elitch Gardens netted $30,000 in the first season, but John died less than a year after the opening. His widow, Mary, continued the project and could be seen riding around the gardens in an ostrich-drawn cart trimmed with flowers.

Amusement park enthusiasts will relish such rides as Mr. Twister, one of the country's top-ranked roller coasters. Toy soldiers guard the arch which welcomes big and little kids into Miniature Madness. All visitors can enjoy the nostalgic pictures of famous stars who trod the boards at the oldest continuously operating summer theater in the nation, the famous floral clock that marks both day and hour, and the Old West buildings. Throughout the park grow the flowers of Elitch's, raised in the Gardens' own greenhouse.

Retrace your route from Elitch's via Thirty-eighty, Irving and Speer to Interstate 25 to return to Colorado Springs.

Colorado's Capitol serves as a focal point for one set of downtown attractions, and Larimer Square anchors another set in lower downtown. Park your car and use the Sixteenth Street shuttle to commute between the two areas and to enjoy city shopping. Route One places you in Larimer Square, and Route Two takes you two blocks from the Capitol as you pass the Basilica of the Immaculate Conception.

Its dome finished in real gold leaf and its thirteenth step one mile above sea level, Colorado's statehouse caps a low hill. Builders used many native materials including Colorado granite, sandstone, marble, and a unique rose quartz found nowhere else in the world. The building represents an investment of twenty-two years and three million dollars and features a design similar to the United States Capitol. Gold leaf coats the dome of the 272-foot building. Colorado miners donated the first gold at the time of construction, and subsequent sheathing restores the original luster.

Traditionally the Capitol's thirteenth step has proclaimed its location as "one mile above sea level." But in 1969 some enterprising engineering students from Colorado State University in Fort Collins discovered a computation error and reassigned the honor to a spot three steps higher. Now one finds the double assertion that Denver merits its designation as "The Mile High City." Enter the building to view the murals in the rotunda, the 180-foot dome featuring a stained glass State Hall of Fame, and bronze elevator doors detailing Colorado's history.

At Thirteenth and Broadway find Colorado Heritage Center. Custodian of the state's story, the Colorado State Historical Society maintains research facilities, western exhibits and changing displays at the Center. A Colorado Chronicle provides a time line of the state's development. See a windmill and mining equipment, dioramas and an extensive collection of pictures by the pioneer photographer, William H. Jackson.

Across Broadway on Fourteenth the Denver Art Museum's gray glass tile walls rise like a castle's battlements. To detail the basic statistics — seven stories, twenty-eight sides, one million tiles, seven curatorial departments, 30,000 art objects — provides dull stuff in contrast to the dynamic reality that is the Denver Art Museum. Spacious and specialized galleries on six floors and the mezzanine display fine arts, crafts and anthropological pieces from prehistoric to contemporary times. Treasures from Europe, Asia, Africa, and the South Pacific share the museum with art from the Americas. Small buildings and period rooms enliven displays from the days of chivalry and colonial times.

Denver's City and County Building provides the western bracket defining Civic Center Park, and the State Capitol forms its eastern boundary. Within the park find the Greek Theater, statues and a sweeping view of downtown's skyscrapers. Denver's tallest building misses by

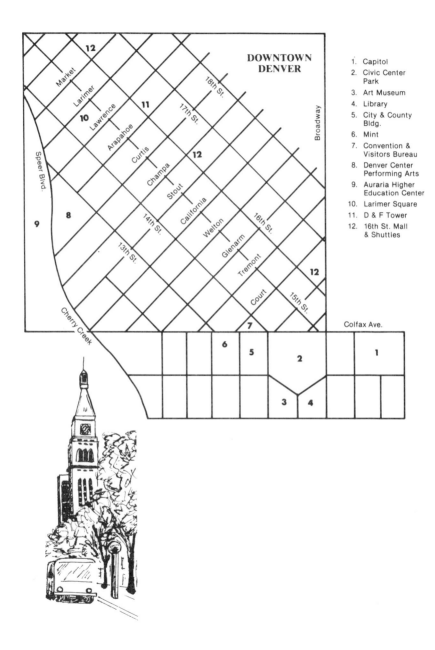

DOWNTOWN DENVER

1. Capitol
2. Civic Center Park
3. Art Museum
4. Library
5. City & County Bldg.
6. Mint
7. Convention & Visitors Bureau
8. Denver Center Performing Arts
9. Auraria Higher Education Center
10. Larimer Square
11. D & F Tower
12. 16th St. Mall & Shuttles

Market
Larimer
Lawrence
Arapahoe
Curtis
Champa
Stout
California
Welton
Glenarm
Tremont
Court
18th St.
17th St.
16th St.
15th St.
14th St.
13th St.
Speer Blvd.
Broadway
Cherry Creek
Colfax Ave.

only nine inches the maximum height allowed because of the flight path to Stapleton International Airport.

Behind the City and County Building, at West Colfax and Cherokee, locate the Denver Mint. Begun as an assay office in 1862, the site became a coinage mint in 1906 and ranks second only to Fort Knox as a repository for the nation's gold bullion. In fact, in the summer of 1983 two air force transport planes, followed by five semi-trailer trucks, conveyed over 8,000 gold bars worth $1.4 billion to the Mint from San Francisco. A mid-1980s expansion ups the Mint's daily production to 35 million coins.

Since its completion in 1982, the vehicular-restricted mall on Sixteenth Street has proved to be a success with both shoppers and merchants. Landscaping, seating areas, entertainers, vendors, and festivals enhance this downtown attraction. Shuttle buses carry passengers between Broadway and Market Street.

One block from the eastern end of the mall, the Brown Palace Hotel fills the triangle created by Broadway, Seventeenth and Tremont. Mining magnate Henry C. Brown built his "palace" in 1892. Later owners included Winfield Scott Stratton and Horace Bennett of Cripple Creek fame and Denver's Claude Boettcher. The Brown merits a visit as one of Colorado's grand old hotels; it is especially festive at Christmas.

Across Tremont from the Brown, the 1880 Navarre building boasts a Museum of Western Art, the latest in a checkered history of uses. In 1880 a Collegiate Institute for young ladies opened in the four-story building.

By 1890 new owners began a fancy Victorian hotel. Then came the Navarre, first for gambling and ladies of the evening, later for fine dining.

At Fourteenth and Curtis stands the Denver Center for the Performing Arts. The $40.5 million complex features an 80-foot high, one block long glass arch, theaters and the Boettcher Concert Hall, consolidating facilities for all the performing arts. *(You can reach the Auraria campus from the Speer Boulevard side of the Denver Center as well as from Larimer Square.)*

Skyline Park stretches between Fifteenth and Eighteenth on Arapahoe and features the historic Daniels and Fisher tower. Created as an appendage to the early twentieth-century D&F drygoods store, the 1910 tower copies the campanile in Venice. Its 325-foot height made it the third highest building in the country. Consolidating two bits of Colorado history, Daniels and Fisher merged with the May Company from Leadville to become May-D&F.

Between Sixteenth and Seventeenth and from Arapahoe to Larimer stands the 1984 Tabor Center. Commemorating H.A.W. Tabor, the Leadville shopkeeper turned silver king, the center encompasses the site of Haw's Tabor Block. Not only was the 1879 building Denver's tallest (five stories), it also contained the city's first elevator and the Tabor Theater. The modern mixed-use project furnishes space for offices, hotel and shopping galleria.

Sakura Square begins at Nineteenth and Lawrence. This Japanese center hosts oriental shops, businesses, restaurants, gardens and a Buddhist church.

Denver's Union Station, at the foot of Seventeenth, functioned as a famous terminal during the railroad era. Between 1906 and 1932 visitors arrived to find a huge arch, electrically lighted and bidding "Welcome." Presidents, performers, sports figures, and military heroes walked, danced and rode through the arch.

A second proposed route through Denver continues north on Colorado Boulevard from the conclusion of Highway 83. Drive on Colorado past Seventeenth Street to Montview and turn left into City Park by the Museum of Natural History.

Denver's 1900 Museum of Natural History ranks as one of the finest natural history museums in the world and among the largest United States museums. Some seventy amazingly realistic, painstakingly detailed dioramas show the world's animals in their native habitats. Add superb collections of butterflies, minerals and Native American artifacts, plus reassembled dinosaur skeletons and anthropological exhibits. Also quartered in the museum find Gates Planetarium, with star shows and laserium, and IMAX Theater, where the viewer partakes of the action on a screen over four stories high and six wide.

Continue to Denver's Zoo which has been in business since 1896. It pioneered the concept of exhibits with natural surroundings and no bars by building Bear Mountain, the first such display in the United States. The 76-acre zoological park provides homes for 1,600 animals representing 365 species.

Turn left from the park onto Twenty-third, cross York to the next street, Gaylord, and turn left. In the middle of the block on the left stands the mustard-colored Pearce-McAllister Cottage bordered by a white picket fence.

Frederick J. Sterner, architect of Colorado Springs' second Antlers Hotel and originally hired for the Broadmoor, designed this Colonial Revival house in 1899. Harold V. Pearce, manager of the Argo Smelter, married a daughter of Dr. and Mrs. William A. Bell of Manitou. Henry McAllister, son of the major whose home became the McAllister House Museum in Colorado Springs, purchased the cottage in 1907. Members of the McAllister family owned the house until 1970 when it passed to the Colorado Historical Society. Don't miss the white cast iron cat crouched at the peak of the gambrel roof!

Drive on Gaylord to Sixteenth and turn right. Continue sixteen blocks to Pennsylvania Street and turn left. The twin towers of the Basilica of the Immaculate Conception extend the building 210 feet into the sky. Both soft gray limestone exterior and Carrara marble interior serve as a background for all the ornate grandeur of the French Gothic cathedral style: arches, vaulting, tracery, and stained glass. *(At this point you are only two blocks from the Capitol.)*

Continue three streets south on Pennsylvania and find the Molly Brown House, number 1340, on your left. Short on formal education but with an enormous zest for life, Margaret Tobin came from Missouri to Leadville and married James Joseph Brown. Along with a wealth of legends which developed following her death in 1932, Mrs. Brown acquired the nickname "Molly" and J.J. that of "Leadville Johnny."

With a fortune from the Little Jonny Mine, the Browns moved to Denver and purchased this existing 1889 house, embellished the exterior and completed the interior with ornate Victorian furnishings. In 1970 demolition threatened the House of Lions' future, but Historic Denver, Inc., organized and rallied to save it. After extensive research, renovation went forward according to 1910 photographs. Removing layers of wallpaper and paint unearthed the original wall coverings and colors.

Mrs. Brown traveled widely in Europe, charmed royalty and nobility with her spontaneous friendliness, and learned to speak several languages fluently. Having enjoyed Egypt with the John Jacob Astors, she decided to join them on the *Titanic*. The high point of her story came when the presumably unsinkable steamship sank with great loss of life. She helped row her lifeboat and sang songs to keep up flagging spirits. After being rescued, she used her multi-lingual ability to assist surviving immigrant women and children and raised $7,000 for them. These efforts and her remark to a New York reporter that she was unsinkable made her a national heroine, and now her story carries the title "The Unsinkable Molly Brown."

Continue five blocks south on Pennsylvania, passing many fine old restored mansions. Just south of the intersection of Pennsylvania and Eighth Avenue locate a small park separating the Grant-Humphreys Mansion to the left and the Governor's Mansion to the right.

Commissioned by Colorado's third governor, James Benton Grant, and completed in 1903, the classical Grant-Humphreys house sports a columned portico. Following Grant's death, mining magnate Albert E. Humphreys bought the home and added a garage large enough to accommodate his ten automobiles.

Mr. and Mrs. Claude K. Boettcher acquired the present chief executive's home in 1923. Claude's father, German immigrant Charles Boettcher, started a hardware store in Fort Collins in 1873. By 1884 he had been instrumental in developing Great Western Sugar Company, Ideal Cement Company, the first meat packing plant west of Chicago, and the largest hardware business in Colorado. He owned the major bank in Leadville and served as trustee of its Mining and Stock Exchange. Claude expanded the family fortune through his investment banking firm and created the Boettcher Foundation to provide millions of dollars for Colorado people and projects.

The Foundation presented the 1908 mansion to the state in 1959. Included were the contents: art treasures and antiques from around the world. At the rear of the house a spacious conservatory with large picture windows extends out toward the gardens. The still predominately white furnishings reflect Mrs. Boettcher's habit of accessorizing the neutral background with colors that matched the party gown she wore. A chandelier from the White House hangs in the drawing room. School children raised money to purchase the silver service and flatware from the USS Colorado after the battleship's decommissioning.

Next on the tour comes Cheesman Park. Walter Scott Cheesman, with a fortune in utilities and real estate, envisioned the future Governor's Mansion in 1901 but died before its completion. Since Eighth is a one-way street west, you must return to Ninth to drive east ten blocks into the park. Follow the curving road to the right as it winds south, east and north to reach the Greek Pavilion and rose gardens. Continue past the pavilion, then bear right to Eleventh Avenue and drive east four blocks to a right turn on York. Watch for an immediate left turn into the parking lot for the Denver Botanical Gardens.

The Botanical Gardens advertises "a place where plants and people grow." Established in 1951 and ranging over twenty landscaped acres, the gardens border a grand old residential neighborhood and Cheesman Park. Trees and shrubs, ground covers and flowers, herbs and vegetables combine with streams, fountains, waterfalls, and pools to form theme areas such as rose, alpine, Japanese, and Scripture gardens. A spectacular conservatory highlights Boettcher Memorial Center, also housing an orchid pavilion, education center and gift shop.

Exit the Botanical Gardens parking lot back to York and turn left. As it crosses Cherry Creek, York becomes University Boulevard. Continue south on University across Alameda and four blocks more to a right turn onto Exposition Avenue. In eight blocks Exposition reaches Washington Park. On the left you will see Eugene Field's cottage and a marble statue of Wynken, Blynken and Nod from his beloved children's poem.

Eugene Field worked on the *Denver Tribune* from 1881-83. There he pioneered his journalistic specialty, a personal column of humorous observations plus literary and dramatic criticism. He went on to become famous as both columnist and poet. Molly Brown bought this tiny cottage for the many generations of children who have dreamed over Field's gifts to them.

Turn right within the park and follow the road as it rounds the north end of a lake and continues along the west side of the park. Pass Washington Park's well-known flower gardens and turn right to Downing Street. To return to Colorado Springs turn left and find Interstate 25 in one-half mile.

45

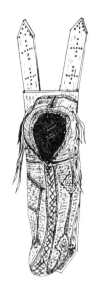

Plains Indians lived on America's grasslands at least ten thousand years before the scant timespan of 1800-1870 that created the classic picture of a warlike, nomadic, mounted buffalo hunter in feather headdress and body paint, breechcloth and moccasins, wielding bow, arrows and warclub.

Even babies adapted to the Native Americans' nomadic life, being transported by cradleboard in a decorative case attached to two pieces of wood. An Indian mother speaks:

The board and the footrest are sunbeams
The canopy is the rainbow;
*   the buckskin lacings are zigzag lightening.*
The children are wrapped in clouds
*   with pillows of mirage and heat.*

The buffalo constituted a department store on the hoof for Plains Indians, who used every part of the animal for food, lodging, clothes, tools, or equipment. Buffalo rawhide created the parfleche, a large folding container used to store food or as a suitcase, and circular shields. Tanned skins made tipi covers and clothing. A hard bone sliver served as a needle and the spongy, porous part of the legbone as a paintbrush. The list seems as endless as the prairie skies.

The patriotic fervor of a young nation's Manifold Destiny removed in less than a century what 10,000 years had failed to destroy. Westward expansion pushed the Native Americans farther and farther toward the Shining Mountains. Settled groups became nomadic hunter and warrior communities. Intertribal warfare accelerated. Cholera, whooping cough and measles decimated susceptible native populations. White buffalo hunters gunned down their bison. Treaties made to be broken took their land. The benevolent Great Father in Washington sought only to civilize the red man, that is, to make him a literate, English-speaking farmer. And the sun set on the free warriors who had mastered, but also had been good stewards of, the great High Plains.

HIGH PLAINS

ONE TRIP ON WHEELS EAST

This section features the High Plains of eastern Colorado. Remember that the land where most of the Front Range cities now stand once gave the same dry, treeless appearance. Trees appeared only near water until developers planted them by the thousands.

The coming of the Combined Space Operations Center in the 1980s and the spurt of growth east from Colorado Springs continue to push back the prairie's western edge. However, this tour puts you on roads where you still can enjoy the wide open spaces with wildflowers, domestic and native animals, and the geological surprise of Calhan Paint Mines.

If you wish to spend more time exploring than this trip requires, an option that includes Castlewood Canyon State Park and the towns of Elizabeth and Elbert precedes the regular tour. Another possibility adds the Arkansas Valley trip to this one; turn east instead of west at the intersection of Calhan Highway and Colorado 94 and head toward Yoder.

Mileage: 100 miles   *Actual driving time: 2½ hours*

Call it the grassland, the plains, the prairie. More than one-third of Colorado's total acreage marches across the eastern flatlands. The High Plains form the western boundary of the vast "Sea of Grass" that flows from the central United States to the foot of the Rockies.

Ancient geological eons witnessed an intriguing parade of events across the present High Plains. Oceans, mountains, forests, and glaciers arrived and departed. Trapped inland seas dried up when the Ancestral Rockies thrust up through the earth's crust only to be eroded in time. Tropical hardwood forests yielded to the savanna pattern of grass interspersed with trees after the uplift of the present Rockies. The mountains cut off the flow of moist Pacific air, and savanna became grassland with trees remaining only near water. Cold took its turn as frozen glaciers pushed phlegmatically south during the Ice Age, leaving tundra-like plants behind when they receded. To add to the mosaic of plant life, in a post-Ice Age climate warmer than the present, southwest desert species appeared. Gradually and finally, the High Plains developed as a treeless, semi-arid, level land.

Vast herds of buffalo in the countless thousands thundered across the open prairie. Humanity arrived in the loose amalgam of Native American tribes known as the Plains Indians. Arapaho, Cheyenne, Apache, Comanche, Kiowa, Pawnee, and Sioux followed the bison and the seasons in a nomadic existence. Dogs assisted in transporting tipis and other belongings.

47

European exploration began when Coronado led a 1540 expedition from Mexico City to as far east as the present state of Kansas. Plains Indians inherited a positive legacy from the Spaniards by acquiring the horse, much stronger and more versatile than their dogs and the means to far more sophisticated techniques of hunting and warfare.

Bad publicity from Major Stephen H. Long's exploration in 1820 carried a poor image of the High Plains to the East. Reports called the area "The Great American Desert." Passing it off as a region fit only for buffalo, Long declared that the shortages of wood and water created obstacles that emigrants could not overcome.

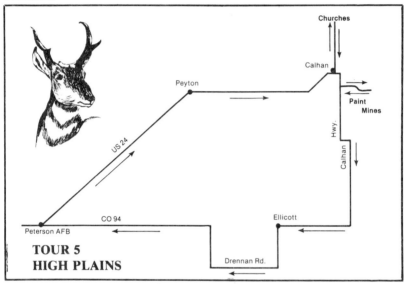

Churches

Calhan

Peyton

Paint Mines

US 24

Hwy.

Calhan

CO 94

Ellicott

Peterson AFB

**TOUR 5
HIGH PLAINS**

Drennan Rd.

Wheels rolling westward did, however, open the High Plains to settlement. First came the prairie schooners, cumbersome and slow, but capable of moving families to the new land. Under the Homestead Act of 1862, the head of a family or someone over twenty-one years of age could claim 160 acres. President Lincoln signed the act into law, but the Civil War delayed movement to the grasslands. When land claimants finally arrived, they found a harsh existence. Hot winds and droughts seared crops in summer. Cold winds and blizzards froze people and animals in winter. Plagues of grasshoppers devastated plantings. Free-ranging cattle encroached on farm lands. The treeless plains left only blocks of sod or sun-dried adobe bricks for buildings. Farmers scratched a meager living from an unfriendly land that yet held a stark beauty and seemed like a desert blossoming in a rainy year.

Ranchers shared prairie land with farmers. Although drives of Texas longhorns trailed to Colorado during the Denver gold boom, the Civil War postponed the main migration. Then the surplus of beef in Texas and the demands of hungry eastern markets combined to make Colorado the end of two cattle trails. The plains provided highly nutritious grasses to fatten the stock, and cattlemen appropriated vast acreage for grazing. A new ease of shipping arrived with the Iron Horse. Silver rails running west from Kansas and south from Denver linked the grasslands to the population centers.

48

Shortly after barbed wire arrived in the 1880s to penetrate cattle country lore, the windmill became a logo for High Plains farmers. Like a giant, many-bladed pinwheel silhouetted against the arching sky, the windmill whirred in the prairie breeze. Far below, a pump raised water from perhaps a hundred feet below ground. And water made the difference between success and failure in this arid land.

Further legislation in the early twentieth century allowed settlers to double and later triple their original 160-acre claims. A time of boom and bust saw World War I and the Depression first escalate and then shatter the hopes of the sod-busters. Homesteaders, aided by new automated farming equipment, stripped prairie surfaces to the bone to raise ever more wheat and corn for war and post-war efforts. With the Depression came not only a drop in corn prices but also the ruinous Dust Bowl years. Farmers had plowed up the natural vegetation that held the soil in place, and for five years the High Plains became the realm of ceaseless, scorching, capricious winds that transported and rearranged the dirt at will. After the mid-1930s government agencies cooperated in the long, frustrating job of resodding the plains. Today traveling irrigation systems tackle the age-old problem of insufficient water, and the High Plains once more host crops and critters on the still wide open land.

ᏋᎶᏋ HIGH PLAINS OPTION ᏋᎶᏋ

If you are coming from Denver, or if you would like a more diverse view of the eastern grasslands, begin the High Plains tour at Franktown on Colorado Highway 83. Located thirty-five miles north of Colorado Springs or thirty-one miles south of Denver, Franktown's historic marker introduces J. Frank Gardner, an 1859 pioneer settler. The town that bears his name served as a way station on the stagecoach line between Denver and Santa Fe. From Franktown, add fifty-three miles and one and one-half hours to the tour.

The approach from Colorado Springs allows you a preview of Castlewood Canyon State Park as you cross the bridge over Cherry Creek five miles south of Franktown. This same Cherry Creek yielded the first Colorado gold in 1858 and led argonauts to Denver. Rugged canyon walls and a variety of vegetation punctuate the landscape on both sides of the highway.

To reach the park proper continue to Franktown and turn west on Colorado Highway 86 across Cherry Creek. Turn left on Douglas County Road 51 and drive two miles straight ahead (do not turn right on Willow Lake Drive) *to Castlewood Canyon State Park. A rough dirt road leads you on the three-mile drive through the park. Hiking trails allow a more detailed look if time permits.*

The 873-acre, day-use park features the 90-foot deep canyon with its creek and small waterfall. Scrub oak and evergreens share the landscape with leafy cottonwoods. Note the ruins of an 1890 dam, originally built to provide flood control as well as irrigation for nearby cherry orchards.

49

A popular recreation spot for turn-of-the-century Denverites, the canyon fell into disuse after the dam's collapse in 1933. However, residents aware of the canyon's beauty encouraged Colorado's initial land purchase in 1961. The state acquired eighty acres from Lawrence Brown, son of the Unsinkable Molly.

Retrace your route from the park back to Franktown. Cross Highway 83 and continue east on Highway 86. Look to the right for some long-range views of Pikes Peak framed by ponderosa pines.

Nine miles east of Franktown reach the town of Elizabeth. Like so many eastern Colorado communities. Elizabeth grew up when the railroad came. John Evans, second governor of Colorado Territory, promoted the town and named it for his sister-in-law. Evans gave his name to Evanston, Illinois, and founded Northwestern University. Today's Elizabeth is developing into an art colony.

Continue six miles east, almost to Kiowa. Turn right on Road 25-41, following the signs to Elbert. This road features a view of the plains that contrasts with the flat, treeless landscape east and south. Here find gently rolling hills and small creeks with their accompanying deciduous trees. Note real, old-fashioned haystacks, looking like great loaves of bread.

A book of the same title speaks of "white churches of the plains." In Elbert, find one of these simple houses of worship on the right as you enter town and another one block left of the highway.

Nine miles south of Elbert on the left side of the road watch for the elaborate Broken Spur Ranch with its longhorn cattle. South of the ranch enter the flat sweep of plains. Drive four miles to Murphy Road; turn left three miles to Peyton Highway and turn right one mile to Highway 24 to meet the High Plains tour.

ⲉⲬ⳥ HIGH PLAINS TOUR ⲉⲬ⳥

Begin this tour by driving east on US Highway 24 from Peterson Boulevard, seven miles east of downtown Colorado Springs.

Highway 24 follows the Rock Island Railroad tracks completed from Limon in 1888, the occasion for founding towns along this road. Between Peyton and Calhan, Big Sandy Creek parallels the highway not far to the north. Indians coming from the plains followed the creek on their way to Manitou's springs and Ute Pass. Early ranchers used the same route to drive cattle to railroad camps where workers lay tracks through the mountains.

In, on and over the open country of the High Plains resides a busy community of life long since banished from urban centers. Defined ecologically as the grassland biome (determined by the predominance of non-woody plants) or as the Upper Sonoran life zone (determined by altitude or latitude), the prairie begins its cycle of life with soil, air, sunshine, and moisture to nourish its plants. Grass eaters like jackrabbits and cottontails in turn make a meal for predators such as coyotes and foxes. Eventually, insects finish the job of decomposition, returning life to the non-living earth to begin the endless cycle once more.

Blue grama and buffalo grasses highlight the native plants of the prairie. Both are noted for the density with which they grow, compacting sod and root systems. Blue grama flies a distinctive purplish-blue flag that dries to a hook shape in fall, and buffalo sports curly gray-green leaf blades. Grama's rich protein content makes it the ideal natural forage whether ripe in summer or dried in winter.

An old cowboy melody sings of "silver on the sage." The silvery gray clumps of pasture sage, although not the sage used in cooking, give off a pungent aroma, particularly when you crush a few leaves between finger and thumb. Pasture sage, like many wildflowers, indicates that overgrazing has allowed other plants to intrude among the native grasses.

Arrive at Calhan, "the highest (6,507 feet) incorporated non-mountain town in North America." The Rock Island founded Calhan, largest of its water stations or "tank towns" along Big Sandy Creek, and built it into a thriving community. Today fifty percent of its residents commute to Colorado Springs as smaller tracts of land replace farming and ranching. However, Calhan continues to serve as a business center for the rural area. The raising of wheat, beans, corn, hay, and alfalfa continues as do dairy, cattle, sheep, and horse operations.

Drive about one mile into Calhan, watch for the airport sign and turn left on the next street, Cheyenne. A very short stretch of dirt road yields

51

to paved Calhan Highway heading straight north out of town. Note the airport with its small planes and in the distance a little church crowning the hill. Just below the steepled church you will see what appear to be two silver silo tops. In fact, you are looking at a second Eastern Orthodox church. Even if you are not intrigued by the sight of two Eastern Orthodox churches in a small Colorado prairie town, the short detour on a good road provides a fine chance to see the reaches of the High Plains. Pikes Peak shimmers on the horizon to the west.

Continue to St. Mary's Church with its two silver, onion-shaped domes and three distinctive Eastern crosses. Drive to the second church where rows of crosses march through a small burial ground to the left. Both churches follow the traditional east-west orientation, with the altar to the east.

Across the street in St. Michael's Cemetery look for Eastern European names on the headstones. Many Slav, Slovak, Serb, and Croat settlers came to the region in the early days of homesteading.

For a convenient turning-around spot, drive over the hill less than a mile to the El Paso County line. Note many yucca plants on both sides of the road. Also known as Spanish bayonet, yucca forms clumps of stiff, sharply-pointed leaves. Stalks of white flowers bloom late in June, and brown, rigidly-dried seed pods rise from the center throughout the year. Yucca blossoms every other year, pollinated by the small white pronuba moth.

Retrace your route to Highway 24; turn left for two blocks, then turn right on Calhan Highway headed south. In less than one-half mile you will see on the right the home of the El Paso County Fair, held each July. In 1983 the Colorado State Rodeo Association voted it the best all-around fair and rodeo in the state.

Turn left immediately past the fairgrounds on Paint Mine Road. Proceed for two miles on the well-graded dirt road and stay left where the road forks. At once watch for a rough road to the left just before a cattle guard. Follow it as it winds downhill to the right to a small parking lot overlooking the Paint Mines, a totally unexpected geological mini-wonder amid the plains flatness. *(If the road is wet, you would do well to park on top and walk down.)*

Local opinion avers that the Plains Indians used the colored clays to make paint. It also appears that Artus Van Briggle of pottery fame tried the Paint Mines as a source for his materials. Even today a Denver brick and tile company takes out clay from the privately-owned acreage.

Geologists call the startling formations "hoodoos." Weathering of soft layers of rock results in the colorful pinnacles that suggest raspberry and apricot sherbets topped with dollops of whipped cream. The Paint Mines cover a limited acreage and gullies between the hoodoos are not deep so exploration can be short and simple. Try to take time to go below and enjoy the vivid colors against the high, wide and blue prairie sky.

Return to Calhan Highway; turn left and continue about six miles to a stop sign. Following the directions to Yoder, turn left on Judge Orr Road for two miles and then right on Calhan Highway. Again during this portion of the tour watch for wildlife of the grasslands along with domestic cattle. Although the bison has vanished from its original domain, you can still see the American pronghorn. This unique animal occupies a family of its own although it suggests the true antelope of Africa. Its horns, composed of fused hair, resemble the rhino's, and the pronghorn sheds the outer sheath each year. No horse can catch the fleetfooted pronghorn. Indians formed a scattered circle around the herd and chased animals back and forth within it until the prey tired. As the circle gradually tightened, hunters came close enough to use bow and arrow.

Once proud monarchs of the plains, American bison boasted a western population of sixty million in 1800. By 1890 less than two thousand remained. Bison served as food for railroad workers, pleasure targets for hunters and railroad travelers, fur coats and robes, and a source for leather. William F. Cody (Buffalo Bill) shot 4,280 bison in one eighteen-month period. To an expanding America, removal of the bison meant removal of the often feared and hated Indian. A Kiowa legend tells of the Great Spirit promising the animals for food and clothing but adds, "In the day that the buffalo shall perish, that day the sun shall set upon the Kiowa."

Bison measured up to six feet in height at the shoulders and could weigh a ton. In the early 1800s a young soldier on his first trip west thought he was seeing elephants when the bulls stampeded. In 1902 Yellowstone National Park provided a home for thirty survivors, and the buffalo narrowly escaped extinction.

Drive south on Calhan Highway to State Highway 94 and turn right, back toward the mountains. Continue about seven miles to the town of Ellicott. Turn left on Ellicott Highway by the Dickinson Ranch, one of the largest longhorn cattle ranches in the country. Dickinson furnished the Texas longhorn on display at the Prorodeo Hall of Fame in Colorado Springs. The ranch provided a "first" at the State Fair in 1983 when it displayed Ankole Watusi longhorns from the Congo, the world's oldest known breed of cattle.

Go six miles south on Ellicott Highway to Drennan Road. The Consolidated Space Operations Center makes Drennan a major thoroughfare from Colorado Springs to CSOC, but here you still can smell the flowers and hear the birds. Turn right on Drennan to step back into the days of the sodbusters. Collapsing buildings and windmills and old Drennan School all remind one of abandoned dreams in the tough, harsh reality of High Plains life. Birds seem to appear on every fencepost. You may see anything from eagle, hawk or prairie falcon to the black and white lark bunting, Colorado's state bird.

Turn right on Peyton Highway, drive one mile to Enoch Road, turn left and follow Enoch for nine miles. Pass Falcon Air Station, site of the Consolidated Space Operations Center. Ground breaking came in 1983 for the facility that headquarters all Department of Defense space activities. With the North American Aerospace Defense Command's space surveillance already based in Colorado Springs, locating CSOC here logically followed.

Continue to Highway 94, turn left and drive ten miles west to Peterson Boulevard. Turn left to the main gate of Peterson Air Force Base. Continue on Peterson about one mile to Ent and turn left. Outdoor displays of aircraft and missiles front the Edward J. Peterson Museum on the left. The free, small museum also serves as Visitors Center for NORAD, since the public may not tour the Cheyenne Mountain site. See a movie on NORAD and find exhibits about the old Ent Air Force Base (now the Olympic Training Complex) and Peterson Field, Alexander Aircraft, flying "aces" of local interest, and information on space programs.

Return to Highway 24, turn left and proceed into Colorado Springs to complete the tour.

RIVERS AND VALLEYS
FIVE TRIPS ON WHEELS SOUTH

This section takes the traveler southeast, south and southwest of Colorado Springs.

Visit four Colorado valleys: Arkansas, Wet Mountain, Cuchara, and San Luis. Meet two of the state's major rivers, the Arkansas and the Rio Grande. View the world's highest suspension bridge at the Royal Gorge and North America's highest sand dunes at Great Sand Dunes National Monument. Range from the Sangre de Cristos, the Wet Mountains and the Spanish Peaks to populated centers such as Pueblo, Canon City and Trinidad. See busy ranching and farming communities and small towns scarcely touched by time. Include Fort Garland and Bent's Old Fort National Historic Site.

Be aware that if you have extra days, you can easily combine two or more tours. For example, the High Plains trip leads into the Arkansas Valley and the valley into Pueblo. Canon City lies west of Pueblo on Highway 50. By reversing the Cuchara Valley tour and beginning with Trinidad, you can add on the San Luis Valley.

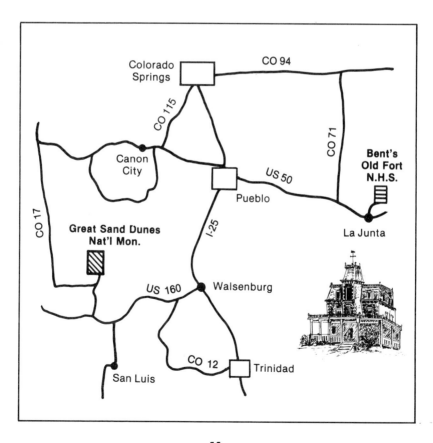

THE ARKANSAS VALLEY

A trip to the Arkansas Valley just before mid-August will catch the last summer performances of the Koshare dancers in La Junta and the first fruits of the harvest at roadside stands in Rocky Ford and Swink. Bent's Old Fort stays open all year, but the Koshare dancers perform only from late June until almost the middle of August and at Christmas.

The Arkansas Valley tour cannot match the variety of Denver and Colorado Springs or the breathtaking mountain scenery, but a day spent with plains, valley and river brings pleasurable experiences. On one research trip we passed a man driving a four-mule, gypsy-type wagon from Minnesota to Arizona, enjoyed a Buck Burshears welcome at the Koshare Museum, and loaded the car's trunk with freshly harvested produce.

Keep in mind the High Plains information as you drive from Colorado Springs to Ordway. Expect summer heat, since daytime temperatures can exceed 100 degrees. Tree-shaded City Park in La Junta makes a nice picnic spot.

Mileage: 240 miles   *Actual driving time: 5½ hours*

The Arkansas River begins in Colorado's Rockies near Leadville, flows south along the mountains, and turns east to cut the Royal Gorge by Canon City. Its meeting with Fountain Creek provides Pueblo's location, and its waters irrigate the farming and ranching country of the Arkansas Valley. The river continues east to Wichita before dropping southeast through Tulsa and Little Rock to reach the Mississippi.

Politically and geographically, the Arkansas River figured prominently in westward expansion. The Louisiana Purchase in 1803 affected land along the Arkansas, since the river served as the boundary between territories of Spain and the United States. Subsequent American expeditions followed its course to explore the new western lands.

Since West Point trained the majority of the country's civil engineers, Army officers usually led the explorations. In 1806 Lieutenant Zebulon Montgomery Pike's party came west along the Arkansas to reconnoiter the situation in Spanish New Mexico.

In 1819 Major Stephen H. Long left St. Louis with instructions to explore the territory from the Mississippi to the Rockies and to permit nothing worthy of notice to escape his attention. The next spring Long's scientific party left the main body and followed the Platte River to the Front Range. Dr. Edwin S. James, Long's botanist, became the first white man to conquer Pikes Peak, and the mountain temporarily carried his name. Once again the company divided, and one group headed home along the Arkansas.

When Mexico gained her independence from Spain in 1821, the northern province of New Mexico began to welcome, and the Arkansas provided access for, American traders. Commerce trailing between Santa Fe and St. Louis sparked a new business network to outfit trappers and handle pelts. Straddling the Santa Fe Trail's Mountain Branch on the river's north bank, Bent's Fort joined the landscape in 1833 as one of the West's most important trading posts.

The Arkansas River continued to function as a major route for westward migration as trails meandering along its banks led soldiers, gold seekers and settlers into the frontier. War with Mexico in 1846 brought Colonel Stephen Watts Kearney's Army of the West to Bent's Fort en route to the conquest of Santa Fe. The river guided Pikes Peak or Bust mining hopefuls. Atchison, Topeka and Santa Fe tracks followed the waterway as the railroad forged west.

Known as "a Santa Fe town," the region's major city, La Junta, provides the valley's commercial center. A townsite mapping occurred in 1876, the year the first Santa Fe train arrived. Incorporation followed in 1881, and location of Santa Fe shops and offices encouraged growth. La Junta is the seat of Otero County, home to Otero Junior College and the Koshare Indian dancers, and closest community to Bent's Old Fort National Historic Site. The Colorado Register of Historic Sites includes its downtown, called "Plaza de Tiempo," as a preservation district.

Belying the Long expedition's dire assessment, the Arkansas Valley sustains cattle ranching and agriculture. Among major crops number alfalfa, corn and sorghum. Speciality crops include onions, beans and tomatoes. The Valley's name is synonymous with succulent melons, and colorful zinnias are raised for seed.

Agriculture began in the valley shortly after the 1859 gold rush, and farmers soon discovered the need for irrigation. Unregulated flow from the Arkansas and its tributaries provided insufficient water so before the turn of the century irrigation companies began building storage reservoirs. Colorado become the first state to supervise water distribution, following the major rivers' natural drainage systems.

Long, painful years of drought led valley residents to appeal for government aid. The Bureau of Reclamation released the Fryingpan-Arkansas water diversion plan in 1953; 1962 saw the project legally authorized. On the Fryingpan River near Basalt begins a series of conduits and tunnels to carry water from the Western Slope to Eastern Slope lakes and reservoirs along the Arkansas River from Leadville to the Arkansas Valley. Increased water benefits include diversification of crops and tripling their yield.

Colorado has been called "The Mother of Waters" or "The Mother of Rivers." Her offspring, the Arkansas, rolls on as it did before the days of Indian and mountain man, trader and explorer, rancher and farmer.

ℰ✦ℓ

Begin this tour by driving east on Colorado Highway 94 from Peterson Boulevard, seven miles east of downtown Colorado Springs via Platte Avenue. Until you reach Calhan Highway, you will be seeing places described in the High Plains tour.

Pass Calhan Highway and on your left note a weathered old barn, considered one of El Paso County's historical sites. Continue east through the small towns of Yoder and Rush. Fifty-six miles from the start of the tour reach Punkin Center, named after a former orange store and gas station.

Turn right on Colorado Highway 71 and proceed forty-six miles to Ordway. Drive another ten miles to the Arkansas River and US Highway 50; turn left to reach Rocky Ford. The town developed at a site where famed scout Kit Carson successfully discovered a ford across the shallow river's rocky bed.

Continue five miles to Swink. The year of 1871 brought George Swink with his family and his seeds to the valley of the Arkansas, beginning the industry that produces some of the world's most delicious melons, Rocky Ford cantaloupes.

The towns of Rocky Ford and Swink also produce vegetable, fruit and flower seeds for international distribution. One catalog lists some forty major families of seeds for edible plants, with over fifteen different varieties of Arkansas Valley cantaloupes. It also includes more than seventy types of flower seeds.

Summer's hot days and cool nights provide the winning combination for growing crops on Otero County farms. The Arkansas Valley Fair, among the oldest in the country, accompanies the August harvest, as does Watermelon Day's giveaway of hundreds of melons.

In addition to agriculture the valley features cattle ranching. Ranches raise cattle for feedlot fattening, an important valley activity; you will see evidence of this business along Highway 50. Buyers and sellers come to La Junta, known as "The Cattle Auction Capital of the Southwestern United States."

Proceed east on Highway 50 through La Junta and follow the signs to Bent's Fort along Colorado Highways 109 and 194. Historians consider the fort to be one of the four major trading establishments in the entire western United States. Efforts of persistent Coloradans brought about the National Park Service's restoration.

Charles and William Bent inherited an involvement with Indians and the new frontier. Their grandfather joined the "Indians" at the Boston Tea Party. Their father served as surveyor-general of the Louisiana Territory with headquarters in St. Louis. When the Bent brothers moved west on the Arkansas River, their chief purpose was trade; however, their presence also assisted their country's expansion.

Trade reached out like tentacles from Bent's Fort. Commerce between St. Louis and Santa Fe passed through the "adobe castle" as did that with Indians and mountain men. Led by the Arapaho, whose very name meant trader, Plains Indians as well as mountain Utes supplied otter, beaver, bear, and muskrat pelts and received weapons, tools, blankets,

kettles, and beads. Trade with Santa Fe involved the exchange of cloth, clothing, food staples, household items, and rum for Mexican gold and silver.

Charles and William Bent joined forces with Ceran St. Vrain, from St. Louis and of French aristocrat background, to create Bent, St. Vrain and Company. By 1840 their trade empire covered much of present-day Colorado and penetrated eight other western and midwestern states.

The Fort provided not only trade, but also protection and a stopping place on the road west. It featured an urbane table with china, crystal, linen, wine, and good conversation. English, Spanish, French, and at least four Indian dialects created a babel of tongues that pervaded the multi-lingual trading post.

The mighty commercial kingdom operated at its peak just before the Mexican War. In the summer of 1846 Kearney's Army of the West arrived at the fort. William Bent aided Kearney's successful, and virtually bloodless, conquest of Santa Fe in August by keeping the Indians neutral.

Disaster came in the latter years of the 1840s. Charles Bent met his death early in 1847 while serving as the first American governor of New Mexico. William Bent and Ceran St. Vrain dissolved the partnership in 1848, and St. Vrain went to New Mexico. The final blow came in 1849 when a severe epidemic of cholera brought by emigrants decimated the Indian tribes. William moved to a new location; whether he blew up the fort or Indians burned it, no one knows, but only ruins remained.

Recognition of the importance of Bent's Old Fort began in 1912 and continued throughout this century, but it took the approach of Colorado's centennial in the same year as the nation's bicentennial to provide the final impetus for reconstruction. Extensive archeological research and historical documentation provided data for the 27,000-square-foot project to begin in 1975. Still surrounded by wide open spaces, the two-story adobe National Historic Site wraps around an inner corral and includes working, living and sleeping quarters; storage, trade and recreation rooms.

Retrace your route to La Junta and proceed on Third Street to Colorado Avenue. Turn left and drive past City Park to Eighteenth Street. Turn right one block to Koshare Indian Museum and Kiva on Otero Junior College campus.

Taking their name from the Pueblo Indian word for a clown, the Koshare dancers are boys from La Junta and Rocky Ford who belong to a Boy Scout Explorer Troop. On July 4, 1983, the communities and his scouts honored J. F. "Buck" Burshears, then 73, for fifty years of volunteer service as Troop 2230's original and only leader. "Buck's Brats" numbered about 3,000 from that half century, and over 500 of them became Eagle Scouts, outdistancing any other troop in the United States. In 1984 Burshears joined eighteen other volunteers who received achievement awards at a White House luncheon.

The Koshare dancers journey nationwide and abroad from this small southeastern Colorado town to portray authentic American Indian dancing. Money raised from the troop's dance performances (over $10 million through the years) built the Koshare Indian Museum. Its collections feature art and artifacts from a variety of North American tribes, an extensive arrowhead assortment and art about Indians. The museum opens year around; the Great Kiva hosts Koshare dancers on selected summer evenings and at Christmas Winter Night Ceremonials, oldest continuous holiday show in Colorado.

Return to Highway 50 and head west for sixty-three miles to Pueblo. Six miles east of Pueblo note the turnoff to the municipal airport. You may enjoy a brief detour to visit the Fred E. Weisbrod Aircraft Museum. Follow the signs to the airport terminal. On your left find numerous aircraft in the large outdoor display dedicated to military airmanship. Transport and combat planes, missile and helicopter share the spotlight with high speed research vehicles tested at the Department of Transportation's facility northeast of the airport.

Return to Highway 50, drive west to Interstate 25 and go north to reach Colorado Springs.

PUEBLO

Pueblo's factory-oriented economy led many Coloradans to consider it an unattractive place to visit. If you have been harboring such thoughts, think again! The city on the Arkansas boasts many attractions. In the summer stop at the little red caboose southwest of Interstate 25 and Highway 50 for information; during the rest of the year go to the Convention and Visitors Bureau at Third and Main, near the Sangre de Cristo Center.

You may choose from a variety of possibilities according to your personal interest. August brings the State Fair, right across from El Pueblo Museum. At any time of year enjoy the parks, see historic mansions in two attractive residential areas, visit the Arts Center, and drive by Colorado Fuel and Iron's massive plant.

If your day permits, add a short drive of some thirty miles southwest on Highway 78 to the delightful mountain town of Buelah and the wooded hills of Pueblo Mountain Park.

Mileage: 110 miles   *Actual driving time: 3 hours*

That attractive attribute, the confluence of two waterways, propelled the site of today's Pueblo into a popular spot for citizens of two nations. Also there came nomadic Native Americans from both plains and high country. Here Fountain Creek's flow from the north meets the Arkansas River journeying east from its mountain source.

A 1706 expedition north from Santa Fe visited the mouth of the Fountain, and its leader acclaimed the broad Arkansas Valley. A century later Pike led his westward survey along the Arkansas and built a log breastwork close to Fountain Creek's flow. Moving north from his encampment at the present site of Pueblo, Pike unsuccessfully attempted to climb the peak that bears his name. His 4,000-foot overestimate of its elevation should have sounded a warning, since the soldiers wore summer uniforms; however, the lieutenant and his party attempted to scale the mountain. November's cold turned back the climbers, and Pike questioned the ability of anyone to make the ascent under such conditions.

The commercial success of Bent, St. Vrain and Company stimulated the creation of a rival trading post called Fort Pueblo. Established in 1842, Pueblo serviced the Trappers' Trail from Taos to Wyoming and had the advantage of being nearer to Taos than any other United States outpost. Taos, though small in size, loomed large in importance as a supply center and as a place for frontier people to receive the sacraments of marriage and baptism. Mexican towns to the south lay much closer than did the United States to the east; two cultures and two languages left their heritage along the Arkansas.

Trailing Kearney's Army of the West came an outfit called the Mormon Battalion, over 300 strong including women and children. From August 1846 until the following spring, this LDS contingent occupied Mormon Town, one-half mile from Pueblo. The city has placed a marker stating that the first white child born in Colorado arrived in Mormon Town.

For several years after the Mexican War Pueblo suffered a series of reversals. The Santa Fe Trail, connecting the United States' new territory to the rest of the nation, lured traffic away from the post. California gold diverted its men to the West Coast. In 1854 Ute Indians massacred all but four occupants.

The valley of the broad, shallow Arkansas coaxed some 1858 Pikes Peak or Bust gold seekers to locate Fountain Village near the river's principal ford. By 1880 a whole collection of settlements existed, with the first houses built from the old trading post's adobe bricks. The town of Pueblo rose on Fountain Creek's west side. South Pueblo developed south of the Arkansas River. Central Pueblo sprang up between the two. The founding of Bessemer came after the steel mill's establishment. Consolidation of the three Pueblos occurred in 1886, and the annexation of Bessemer followed in 1894.

In 1872 General Palmer extended his Denver and Rio Grande from Colorado Springs to Pueblo and across the Arkansas. Southern Colorado coal fields fueled the plants designed to fulfill General Palmer's intent to make Pueblo "the Pittsburgh of the West" and to provide low cost iron and steel products for his railroad. Formation of the Colorado Coal and Iron Company and construction of blast furnaces led to the 1882 Bessemer converter production of the first steel west of the Mississippi. Ten years later a merger created the Colorado Fuel and Iron Corporation, involved with both iron and steel making and the manufacture of rails, rods, wire, spikes, and nails. Having become the West's great iron and steel city, Pueblo boasted a population of 24,000 by 1890, second only to Denver.

Pueblo served as the saddle-making capital of the West.

Today's Pueblo remains an industrial center coupled with modern diversity of historical, agricultural, recreational, and intellectual pursuits and opportunities. Many buildings appear on the National Register of Historic Places. Thousands of visitors throng the Colorado State Fair each August. A dam has caught the Arkansas River's flow to create Lake Pueblo, a reservoir that forms the largest body of water in southern Colorado. The University of Southern Colorado and the Sangre de Cristo Arts and Conference Center headquarter educational and cultural activities.

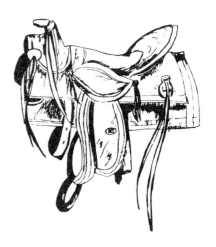

Begin this tour at South Circle Drive and Interstate 25, three miles south of downtown Colorado Springs and almost forty miles north of Pueblo. Drive south on I-25 past Security, Widefield and Fort Carson. Note the turnoff to Fountain, one of the oldest towns in central Colorado and home of Fountain Valley School. Betty Hare, who spearheaded efforts to construct the Colorado Springs Fine Arts Center, also lent her talents to founding this prestigious college preparatory school. Like the Arts Center, Fountain Valley features southwestern art and architecture. Broadmoor's Spencer Penrose served on the first Board of Trustees, as did famed educator John Dewey.

To the left a steady parade of cottonwood trees along its bank marks Fountain Creek's progress south toward Pueblo. After you pass the city limits sign, the fortress-like buildings of the University of Southern Colorado appear on your left. Ahead rise the stacks of Colorado Fuel and Iron Corporation.

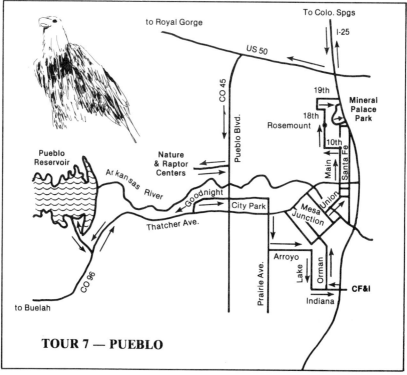

TOUR 7 — PUEBLO

Turn right on US Highway 50, following signs to Canon City and the Royal Gorge. In two miles turn left on Colorado Highway 45 (Pueblo Boulevard). Continue south three miles, then turn right on Eleventh Street where you will see a sign for the Nature Center of Pueblo. Turn right to reach the Nature Center and the Raptor Center of Pueblo.

A recovery facility for injured birds of prey, the Raptor Center provides both short and long term care for such predators as eagles, hawks, owls, and falcons. With problems caused by illness, malnutrition and capture, feathered guests receive visiting veterinary care and regular staff attention. Although the primary object is to return birds to the wild, a few that cannot be released remain at the Center so that visitors may have a first-hand chance to learn about the characteristics, problems and preservation of raptors.

Return to Pueblo Boulevard and turn right. At the first traffic light after crossing the Arkansas River turn right on Goodnight Avenue, drive to Colorado Highway 96 (Thatcher Avenue) and turn right. Note the historic Goodnight Barn immediately past a large concrete plant on the right.

Charles Goodnight became a cattle baron by running Texas longhorns north to Colorado and Wyoming on the trail that bore his name. Cowboys herded five million head of longhorn cattle along the 2,000 miles of Goodnight trails between 1866 and 1884. The old stone barn stands as the last survivor of Goodnight's empire and recalls the legendary days of cattle drive and open range.

Continue past the barn three miles to Pueblo State Recreation Area. Observe the sign for, and drive one-half mile to, park headquarters. You must purchase a day's pass to use the lake, but you may enjoy at no charge the Visitors Center with a film about the reservoir, a collection of Colorado butterflies and a good observation point for activity on the water. Lake Pueblo offers a sharp contrast to the treeless cliffs and plains circling the seventeen-mile shoreline. The Sangre de Cristos rise to the west with Pikes Peak visible across the water to the north. At the east end of the reservoir note the dam that holds water in the largest storage facility of the Fryingpan-Arkansas diversion project.

Retrace your route five miles from the Visitors Center to Highway 96 to Goodnight to Pueblo Boulevard. Continue straight ahead to enter City Park. Follow the one-way road to the right and pass some of the Pueblo Zoo exhibits. The zoo provides a home for over seventy species of animals and features Happy Time Ranch where visitors may mingle with farm stock. Texas longhorns serve as reminders that Goodnight Ranch once covered this acreage.

Also in City Park see the historic carousel, object of a citizens' restoration project. Interested friends of the nostalgic horses and chariots point out that while a merry-go-round rotates in a clockwise direction, the old carousels spin counter-clockwise.

Exit the park on Goodnight Avenue and drive five blocks to Prairie Avenue. Turn right and follow the signs to the State Fairgrounds.

Colorado State Fair and Industrial Exposition delights both state residents and visitors each August. An average 400,000 people enjoy carnival rides and entertainment ranging from American country western to

Mexican fiesta. In addition to the traditional agricultural and livestock displays, attractions include an Industrial/High Technology Center and a Fine Arts Building.

Across the street from the Fairgrounds spot El Pueblo Museum. Housed in an old airplane hanger, the museum features units on exploration, trapping and settlement through dioramas, models and displays. Note the small gold, silver and gemstone model of the late Mineral Palace. You will be driving through Mineral Palace Park at tour's end. The museum centers on a reconstruction of Fort Pueblo and contains a detailed story of iron and steel making from iron ore to manufactured products.

Continue on Prairie to the end of the fairgrounds and turn left on Arroyo. Drive about one mile to Lake Avenue and turn right. Proceed another mile to Indiana and turn left to the Colorado Fuel and Iron Corporation's plant one-half mile away. The end of 1983 saw the end of an era as CF&I, once Pueblo's largest employer and economic base of the city, cut two-thirds of its work force and permanently shut down four blast furnaces. The company continues to use electric arc furnaces to produce steel rails and wire products.

Return on Indiana to the traffic light at Orman and turn right. In one mile follow Orman's diagonal left to enter Mesa Junction district, site of some of the city's fine old mansions. Near the corner of Orman and Colorado stand several homes built before the turn of the century. On your left at that intersection find 102 West Orman. Colorado Governor James B. Orman built the red sandstone dwelling. Alva B. Adams, three times governor and twice U.S. senator, later purchased the home.

Drive on Orman three blocks to Van Buren; turn right for two blocks and turn right onto Pitkin. This 300 block on your right, known as Pitkin Place, carries a National Historic Register designation; note particularly the stone mansion on the far corner.

Continue on Pitkin two blocks to Colorado and turn left. Proceed three blocks, cross Abriendo and drive on Union as it makes a short diagonal right and then turns left toward downtown.

Cross the Arkansas River and see Pueblo Union Station on the left. Manitou red sandstone created the 1889 Richardsonian Romanesque Revival D&RG depot, once among the busiest in Colorado and second in size only to Denver's Union Station. Picture the tower standing twenty feet taller. It was lowered in 1921 for fear that flood waters had weakened the building's foundation. In 1983 a Colorado Springs developer bought the building from four railroads that had not used it since the early 1970s. Conversion centers on shops, offices and restaurants echoing the present use of Colorado Springs depots.

Historic Union Avenue contains many of Pueblo's vintage buildings. Continuing restoration updates the turn-of-the-century structures. Cross Elizabeth to see City Hall and Memorial Auditorium on your right and the 1910 Vail Hotel on your left. Small, triangular Pueblo-Puebla Plaza commemorates the friendship between Pueblo and the city of Puebla in Mexico.

Follow Union to First; turn right for two blocks and turn left on Santa Fe. Proceed one block to the Sangre de Cristo Arts and Conference Center on your right. The Center provides a place for people to see and do visual and performing arts in gallery, theater and experiential class. Built in 1972, the Center celebrated a major addition ten years later and houses the Francis King Collection of Western Art.

Go left on Third one block to Main and turn right to Tenth. Turn left to see Pueblo County Courthouse on your right. Finished in 1912, the building underwent remodeling for Colorado's 1976 centennial. Drive two blocks to Grand and turn right to enjoy churches, synagogue and homes from the late nineteenth and early twentieth centuries.

Find the Thatcher mansion, Rosemount, at the corner of Grand and Fourteenth. John Thatcher came west from Pennsylvania. After he successfully sold wagonloads of goods brought from Denver, he opened a store. The store's safe began Pueblo's First National Bank, and Thatcher became a wealthy man. Five years of planning and two of building preceded Rosemount's completion in 1893. The 37-room mansion's furnishings and decorations frequently repeat rose designs, reflecting Mrs. Thatcher's love of roses. Honeyed oak, curly birch with mother-of-pearl inlay, and mahogany fireplace trimmed in silver retain turn-of-the-century opulence. The third floor houses the Andrew McClelland Cabinet of World Curiosities, an intriguing hodge-podge of collectables from around the globe.

Locate the 1893 red sandstone Queen Anne residence across Fifteenth from Rosemount and continue on Grand to Eighteenth. Turn left one block to Greenwood, then turn right, noting the 1892 stone and brick house with a corner tower. Turn right on Nineteenth and drive three blocks to Main. Turn left into Mineral Palace Park and follow the one-way road around to the right.

Promoters built the Mineral Palace in 1890 to advertise Colorado's great mining industry with a collection of minerals called the largest in the world. The palace enthroned King Coal and Queen Silver; its decorations included mineral mosaics. Deterioration of the building prompted its destruction in the 1940s.

Drive through Mineral Palace Park and exit the opposite side. Turn left to Santa Fe, right to Thirteenth and left to I-25 north to Colorado Springs.

WET MOUNTAIN VALLEY — CANON CITY

This tour verifies the old adage that variety is the spice of life. Journey from the cactus-dotted, desert-like plains south of Florence to the creeks, canyons and conifers of Hardscrabble Pass. Explore the farm and ranch country of the productive Wet Mountain Valley, bastioned by the great Sangre de Cristo Mountains. Marvel at the waters and rock walls of the Arkansas River. Join the fun at Buckskin Joe and cross the Royal Gorge bridge. Take the High Drive to Canon City.

A fourteen-mile side trip on Colorado Highway 165 west of Wetmore offers an unusual option. The Bishop family of Pueblo is building a castle! A young couple's dream of a stone house on their mountain property led to the ongoing construction of the Castle of Golden Hours. This family hobby will have been at least twenty-five years in building before it reaches completion. It will function under a non-profit organization as a museum and a main hall for dances, weddings and fund raisers. The scenic drive, a good one for fall aspen colors, enhances a visit to the castle.

Mileage: 200 miles   *Actual driving time: 4½ hours*

Zebulon Pike's exploration up the Arkansas River provided the first documentation about the Royal Gorge, called "The Grand Canyon of the Arkansas." The 1820s opened the region to trappers, traders and mountain men. Army topographic engineer John Charles Frémont visited during his expeditions in the 1840s. Frémont covered thousands of miles exploring the West under the sponsorship of his father-in-law, Senator Thomas Hart Benton of Missouri.

The 1860s witnessed settlement of Canon City. The Civil War disrupted development as trade routes changed and the population went off to battle. When growth resumed after the conflict, poet Joaquin Miller served as mayor and judge and sought to have the community named Oreodelphia. Residents demurred, asserting that they wanted to be able to pronounce their town's name and to spell it.

General Palmer's Denver and Rio Grande brought rails to Canon. A dispute known as "The Royal Gorge War" erupted over who would control the railroad right of way through the Arkansas River chasm, the favored route from Pueblo to Leadville. Holding opposite ends of the gorge, men of both the D&RG and the Santa Fe lines occasionally fought each other in person while their superiors battled through the courts. A Supreme Court decision ruled in Palmer's favor.

Headquartering such disparate enterprises as the State Penitentiary and a Benedictine abbey, Canon City boasts a diversified economy. Passenger trains no longer run on the Rio Grande line, but freight cars still roll through town. Serving as the seat of Fremont County, the city also functions as business hub to other county communities.

At one time rails connected Canon City to Westcliffe and the Wet Mountain Valley to the south. The few small population centers in Custer County still look to Canon as their "big city."

Cradled between the Wet Mountains to the east and the mighty Sangre de Cristos to the west, Wet Mountain Valley quietly welcomes visitors to a setting of tranquil beauty. Ute Indians relished this lush land that provided plentiful hunting in a protected location. Spanish explorers penetrated the valley and gave the sunset-washed pinnacles the name Sangre de Cristo, meaning "Blood of Christ."

The first settlement in the Wet Mountain Valley occurred in 1870 when several hundred German immigrants came from Chicago to found a community called Colfax, named for the vice president of the United States and located southwest of today's Westcliffe. Their experiment at a communal colony failed, but they stayed on to divide up the land for privately-owned farms and ranches, some still held by descendants of the original homesteaders.

The year of 1870 also saw the first casual prospecting for ore, but the rich mineral deposits eluded miners for two more years. Spring of 1873 marked the beginning of the bonanza years that faded quickly but did not end completely until the collapse of silver abetted the Panic of 1893.

Filling the classic role of the dude come west, wealthy young Englishmen of noble families added a touch of color to the valley. Prodigal in their pleasures and free with their cash, they erected English country estates and fostered fox hunts and afternoon tea.

Begin this tour on Colorado Highway 115, the extension of Nevada Avenue, three miles south of downtown Colorado Springs.

To the left find Myron Stratton Home, a memorial to his father by Cripple Creek gold mogul Winfield Scott Stratton. A site of attractive buildings and spacious grounds, the home provides quarters for senior El Paso County residents and for emotionally handicapped children.

In three miles note the turnoff to the North American Aerospace Defense Command. NORAD, combining air force units of the United States and Canada, maintains its Combat Operations Center inside Cheyenne Mountain. Established in 1957, NORAD's mission comprises surveillance and defense of our continent's airspace.

Across the highway lies Fort Carson, the army's "Mountain Post" named for Kit Carson. Created in 1942, Carson numbered a World War II population of 43,000 and served as a German POW internment camp. The original 60,000 acres has increased more than six-fold to the present time. The post contains a fine Museum of the Army of the West. Ask directions at the main gate.

Continue driving south on Highway 115 to the town of Florence. You may proceed straight ahead to visit the community or continue on your way by turning left on Colorado Highway 67 at a sign for the State Veterans Nursing Home.

Named for the daughter of a senator who incorporated the town in 1887, Florence boasts a unique history involving two fuels. Discovery of the second oil well in the United States occurred near Florence in 1898; coal mining followed as a major industry. Three railroads served this oil refining center which grew larger than Canon City by 1901. Florence has its Main Street, parks, Victorian houses, and Pioneer Museum. Each September the town hosts "Tour de Hardscrabble Pass," a 100-mile bicycle race that follows this tour to Westcliffe and then back via Highway 50.

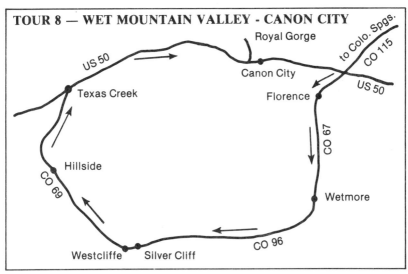

Leave Florence on Highway 67 for the eleven-mile drive to Wetmore. Cacti dot the landscape and oil wells pump. The tiny community of Wetmore nestles east of the San Isabel National Forest. Before continuing west you may want to stop in town. The old general store first served as a stage stop on the Hardscrabble Trail. Now it features a companionable pot-bellied stove and chairs for visitors.

According to local legend, Bob Ford did not kill outlaw Jesse James, and Jesse showed up in Wetmore. The proof? A sign of Jesse's presence, a turkey track mark, appeared in the area.

Go west on Highway 96 and experience a change of scene from the former arid landscape to trees, hills and ranches. Enter San Isabel National Forest and ascend the Wet Mountains via Hardscrabble Pass, a short and easy grade along Hardscrabble Creek. Sources agree that the name Hardscrabble came about from early difficulties of making a living in these parts. *(If you are planning to visit the Bishop Family Castle, watch for the left turn onto Colorado Highway 165 after climbing the pass.)*

Continue on Highway 96 and note the road to the ghost town of Rosita. Rosita flourished for a few brief years in the 1870s after the organization of Hardscrabble Mining District in 1872. The boom town boasted all the usual enterprises plus one of the largest breweries and the first cheese factory in the Territory. Two major silver mines swelled population and produced fortunes. Little now remains to merit a detour.

Driving uphill after the Rosita road gives one a feeling of anticipation for what will be visible from the top of the rise. Within one-half mile that expectation comes true as peaks of the Sangre de Cristo mountain range appear, standing sentinel over the secluded Wet Mountain Valley with its neighboring towns of Silver Cliff and Westcliffe.

Arrive first at Silver Cliff, twenty-five miles from Wetmore. The 1878 discovery of rich silver ore in the thirty-foot high black cliff on your right gave the town its name. Called "horn silver," this chloride assayed up to 75 percent pure silver and caused the meteoric rise of a mining town that grew fast, lived hard and nearly died out in a remarkably short time. Silver Cliff rivaled the Cloud City of Leadville in its sporting life and competed with Denver to become the state capital, barely losing out, residents say, because Denver beefed up its voting roles with names from tombstones. Yet only two years after its great boom season of 1880, Silver Cliff already had started downhill. Mines began closing due to poor management and greedy speculation.

Once a bustling community of some 10,000, "The Cliff" now claims a small population of over 200. However, as one citizen says with a chuckle, "It's a mighty active little ghost town"! Try to visit the historic museum on your left.

Continue from Silver Cliff directly into Westcliffe. The extension of the Denver and Rio Grande from Canon City arrived one mile west of Silver Cliff, creating this new company town. The narrow gauge D&RG Grape Creek Line arrived in the Wet Mountain Valley in 1881 at a high cost of labor and money. General Palmer's associate, Dr. William A. Bell, owned extensive land in the valley and served as vice president of the railroad. Westcliffe takes its name from Bell's hometown in England.

Despite its stable economic base as the supply and business center for surrounding farms and ranches, Westcliffe had troubles of its own as success and slump alternated through the years. Every heavy rain caused disastrous damage to the railroad, including ten washouts in one year, until in 1890 the D&RG picked up its tracks and went home. But by 1900 back came the same railroad from the Texas Creek side with a standard gauge line. The Depression caused a second abandonment in 1937, leaving ranchers and farmers dependent upon truck transportation. Refrigeration of produce became a problem, because railroads carried ice but trucks did not.

World War II increased prosperity, the 1950s brought another slump, and the sixties heralded a new upswing. In addition to the traditional economy of hay crops and registered cattle, the valley now capitalizes on its natural resources, drawing people to the outdoor life at such prime recreation sites as DeWeese Reservoir and Conquistador Ski Area. Westcliffe is a compact little town, easy to explore by car or on foot. Enjoy the picturesque main street, recalling that a city ordinance harking back to the days of wooden sidewalks still forbids throwing cigarettes or cigars on the street. Weathered buildings exist next to colorful shops. Wander the residential blocks, spotting the old homes and churches and the 1891 school. The Sangre de Cristos, here containing four of Colorado's 14,000-foot peaks, rise from the edge of the valley.

Leave Westcliffe on Highway 69 headed north to Hillside and Texas Creek. Pass a sample of the local ranches and once again experience a change of scenery as the landscape becomes more dry and barren with few trees. Then between Hillside and Texas Creek find gently rolling hills, trees and irrigated land.

Reach the junction of Highway 50 at Texas Creek and turn right toward Canon City. This "River Road" between Salida and Canon City follows the Arkansas River. Water and rock cliffs, a train on the historic railroad tracks across the river, and rafts riding the white water all contribute to the River Road experience. Arrive at Parkdale, cross the Arkansas and prepare for the turnoff to the Royal Gorge on the right in less than three miles.

On the way to Royal Gorge Park you will see Buckskin Joe. Buckskin Joe, one of Colorado's earliest mining towns, actually existed west of present day Alma in the 1860s. Leadville's famed Silver King, H.A.W. Tabor, kept the town store and served as its postmaster. The former mining community had long been a ghost town when, in 1957, the art director of Hollywood's MGM Studio decided to construct a movie set with authentic old buildings. The nucleus was Tabor's store from the original Buckskin Joe. Log structures and board sidewalks, saloon and stage stop, sheriff's office and jail help project one back into another era, as do the gunfights staged on the street. Buckskin Joe often provides the setting for western movies and TV programs.

Perhaps the best reason to bridge the Royal Gorge is because it's there. A Texas promoter, motivated to open the gorge to motorists at the top as well as train travelers at the bottom, commissioned a span to be built over the 1,055-foot deep canyon. Two 150-foot high steel towers anchor the world's highest suspension bridge. Finished in 1929 after six months' construction, the bridge stretches almost one-quarter mile, contains 300 tons of galvanized steel cables and cost $250,000. You may drive or walk over the bridge, ride an aerial tram across the chasm or descend into the ravine on an incline railway. A good option is to take the tram across the gorge and walk back over the bridge. As you look down to the river, recall the problems of building a railroad through the Royal Gorge. A famous "hanging bridge" spanned the narrowest part; steel beams inserted into the cliffs suspended tracks above the canyon floor.

Return from the gorge to Highway 50 and turn right. In two miles watch for a turn to the left onto Skyline Drive through the entry arch featuring rocks from around the country. The three-mile, paved, one-way road straddles an 800-foot high hogback and provides numerous pulloffs to enjoy the view to both sides. Canon City lies to the left, and you can see the State Penitentiary from the last overlook before a hairpin turn begins your descent. Convict labor built the road in 1906.

Skyline Drive becomes Floral Avenue at the stop sign on Fifth Street. Continue straight ahead four blocks, turn right on Ninth and drive five blocks to Greenwood. On your left stands the Gibson House, a stone mansion built in 1900 for $30,000 and owned by a lumber dealer. Continue one block to Macon Avenue and turn right. In two blocks, on the corner of Seventh Street, note two of Canon City's beautiful old churches and between Seventh and Sixth, the Courthouse.

At Sixth Street turn left one block, then right on Main Street. Some historic buildings have been razed but many turn-of-the-century structures still remain.

At First Street Main deadends into the State Penitentiary grounds. In January 1863 Jothan Draper purchased a homestead for $250. Five years later he conveyed to the Territory of Colorado thirty of his acres for $300 under "an act to locate and establish a penitentiary." The Territorial Prison created a strong economic base that still exists. Statistics show that the Colorado Department of Corrections accounts for more than twice as many jobs as the city's second leading employer.

A favorite story of Canon City residents tells how the city faced a choice between being the site of the State Penitentiary or of the State University. Assuming that the former would be better attended, they chose the penitentiary.

Turn left on First; drive across Highway 50 and over the bridge spanning the Arkansas River. At the first corner stands the 1884 Robinson Mansion. With a fortune from area gold and silver mining, Lyman Robinson built this home and several business blocks. Circle the property to view one of southern Colorado's finest examples of Victorian architecture.

Return to Highway 50 and turn right. Proceed to Sixth and on the right find the Municipal Museum with the Rudd Stone House and Cabin to the rear. Fully furnished rooms and curatorial assistance make the pioneer homes come alive.

Continue driving east on Highway 50 and find the Visitors Center in the former Denver and Rio Grande terminal to the right between Eighth and Ninth.

Proceed east on Highway 50 to Highway 115. Turn north and return to Colorado Springs to complete the tour.

Mule deer

Rafting on the Arkansas

Royal Gorge Bridge

Covered bridge near Westcliffe

Cripple Creek wagon,
Myron Stratton Home

CUCHARA VALLEY – TRINIDAD

On this tour you will notice a preponderance of Spanish names indicative of the rich Hispanic heritage of this area. For example, Walsenburg is the county seat of Huerfano (Orphan) County and Trinidad of Las Animas (The Souls) County. Huerfano takes its name from a solitary butte and Las Animas from a portion of the Spanish name for the Purgatoire River. La Veta means "the vein" and refers to the mountains' rich mineral veins. Cuchara (spoon) reflects the spoon-shaped valley. Trinidad (Trinity) bears the name of early settler Felipe Baca's daughter.

It seems like a long drive before you begin circling from La Veta to Trinidad, but a scenic and historic adventure, not as well known as many of the other trips, awaits you. The southern mountains present a different panorama than do those to the west.

Fort Francisco Museum in La Veta and Baca House Museum in Trinidad remain open only from Memorial Day until Labor Day.

Mileage: 310 miles   *Actual driving time: 6½ hours*

Trinidad, the southernmost of the state's Eastern Slope cities, presents a microcosm of southeastern Colorado's story. The early 1700s saw Spanish explorers and French traders moving via Raton Pass to and from New Mexico. In 1821 the Mountain Branch of the Santa Fe Trail angled southwest from Bent's Fort to the site of Trinidad on the Purgatoire River and then headed south. Shepherds and their sheep moved in from New Mexico after the Mexican War. Following the Civil War, in 1866, longhorn cattle from Texas crossed Raton Pass.

Although evidence exists of a permanent settlement as early as 1861, Spanish land grant claims delayed the city's incorporation until 1876, the same year as Colorado's statehood. Trinidad headquarters Las Animas County government. Its central historic district carries the name "Corazon de Trinidad" (Heart of Trinidad).

When Kearney's troops made Raton Pass their access to Santa Fe, a topographic engineer noticed outcroppings of coal near the Purgatoire. Thirty years later the Engleville Mine began production of coal and coke and during the 1880s became the largest producer in Colorado. Production in the southern coal field increased six-fold between 1880 and 1890.

Coal heated homes, fueled railroads and industries, and smelted ores. Coke, distilled by heat to become principally carbon, also provided fuel. Mines near Trinidad produced the highest quality coking coal in the state.

Labor problems hit the coal mines when the United Mine Workers called a strike in September 1913. State militia units guarded property, and a tragic confrontation between militiamen and miners took place in April 1914 at Ludlow

Station, eighteen miles north of Trinidad. Six men died, and a fire in the tent colony claimed the lives of thirteen women and children. The UMW immediately dubbed these events "The Ludlow Massacre," and a ten-day "war" raged in the coal fields. When Colorado's governor appealed for federal aid, United States troops replaced the militia. The strike finally ended in December 1914.

Coal production peaked in 1918 at 12.5 million tons, but mine closures followed in the 1920s and 30s. However, with modern demands for fossil fuels, 1980 increased mining to ten million tons. Today coal mines exist chiefly on the Western Slope, but Las Animas County continues to produce in the eastern part of the state.

At about the same time that sheepherders moved near Trinidad in the 1840s, Colonel John M. Francisco first saw the Cuchara Valley. His description was, quite simply, "Paradise." Between US Highway 160 and the Spanish Peaks, in the Cuchara Valley, nestles the small community of La Veta. Here Colonel Francisco and two associates managed large holdings in farming and ranching from their headquarters at Fort Francisco. The adobe fort, begun in 1862, featured the traditional plan of a thick-walled, square building enclosing an open central plaza.

The Spanish Peaks, awesome twin mountains, rise alone and abruptly above the valley floor. Their unique masses led the Indians to name them Wahatoyah (Breasts of the World). Various legends located the homes and treasures of gods, plus the source of all life and of rain-bearing clouds, on their heights. Both Native Americans and Europeans used the peaks as a landmark leading to New Mexico. They became known as Las Cumbres Españolas (The Spanish Peaks) or Huajatolla, the hispanicized version of the old Indian name.

Ranching dominated the Cuchara Valley's economy as the latter part of the ninetenth century moved onward. Coal mines developed to the west. Railroads arrived to haul out the coal. Trains also carried La Veta cattle to a Pueblo meat packing company and hay to feed the mules working in the coal mines.

As the twentieth century unfolded, mining operations and railroad usage slackened, but the heritage of ranching and farming continued. The quiet valley could well boast of being one of the last undiscovered and undeveloped beauty spots of Colorado. It took non-residents, visitors from Texas, Oklahoma and Kansas, to recognize the potential of the Cuchara Valley.

Begin this tour by driving south on Interstate 25 from Colorado Springs to Exit 52, marked for Walsenburg and Great Sand Dunes National Monument.

Hispanic farmers began a small settlement called La Plaza de los Leones, but Walsenburg takes its name from Fred Walsen. A German immigrant and merchant, Walsen laid out the townsite in 1873 after he left the Wet Mountain Valley. The city owes its development to the Denver and Rio Grande and to coal mines supplying Colorado Fuel and Iron in Pueblo.

Drive three miles through town, following signs to US Highway 160 west. In another two miles note the land and lake acreage of Lathrop State Park on the right. Continue eight miles more and turn left on Colorado Highway 12. As you drive the five miles to La Veta, the Spanish Peaks maintain their commanding position over the Cuchara Valley.

Enter La Veta on Main Street and go one block to Francisco Street. Turn right to the parking lot for Fort Francisco Museum. The Fort became known as Francisco's Plaza, usually shortened to "The Plaza." The multi-use structure protected settlers from possible Indian attacks and headquartered not only Francisco's business enterprises but valley commerce as a whole. It even housed the first post office. As time passed and fear of Indians abated, the old fortress opened its walls on two sides. In 1877 railroad depot and businesses relocated north of the fort, transferring the town's center with them.

The 1862 Plaza structures feature a variety of nineteenth century displays. Note the Indian collection and coal mining museum. Also find saloon, school, church, and blacksmith shop. A large, old cottonwood carries the title "The Hanging Tree" and lived up to its name.

Return to Main Street and turn right. Note the 1877 Baptist Chapel on the left and the 1899 Inn on the right. Continue through town and follow Highway 12 out of La Veta.

Just outside of town, notice Grandote golf resort on the left. PGA player Tom Weiskopf knows a good piece of golf real estate when he sees it, and when he saw the Cuchara Valley he decided it was a natural. Developers implemented the decision to build a 27-hole golf course and resort community. In 1984 they broke ground on former ranch land for a 1986 opening. Grandote's name comes from that of an Indian, El Grandote (The Great One), who led his people to a life of peace and plenty at the Spanish Peaks. Apparently everyone from Native American to PGA professional agrees with Colonel Francisco's assessment: "Paradise."

Continue past Goemmer Ranch, home to six generations of the same family since the first immigrant came from Germany over a century ago. The raising of longhorn cattle continues, reflecting the valley's historic use as a stock-raising site. Among the visitors at Goemmer Ranch was the notorious Jesse James, who approved the blacksmithing work done there and promised armed protection in return.

Your route passes very close to West Spanish Peak. Famous in both history and legend, the peaks also represent a unique geologic study. As the Rockies formed, bubbling thrusts of molten igneous rock, or magma, pushed up against layers of sedimentary rocks laid down over eons of geological time. The magma buckled the layers and accomplished a dual intrusion: first, creating a hard core or "stock" within the upthrust sedimentary rocks; second, seeping like fingers into the cracks. Gradually the softer sedimentary rocks eroded, leaving the harder igneous stocks still standing as the Spanish Peaks. In addition to the peaks, dikes remain as testimony to the cracks once filled with magma. These free-standing rock walls range in length up to fourteen miles and in height up to one hundred feet. Their width varies from one to one hundred feet. Some four hundred examples of these dikes make the Spanish Peaks unique in the world and serve as textbook illustrations of this geologic phenomenon. Examples are visible immediately to your left.

Eleven miles from La Veta reach Cuchara. The picturesque town comprises only one long block and allows for easy browsing. Bare wood buildings, plank sidewalks, railings, and hitching posts all combine to resemble a theme park or Western movie set. "Rustic" may be the word for the first overall impression, but the rough facades front modern and gracious shops, galleries, restaurants, and lodging.

Continue up Cucharas Pass, noting the entrance to Cuchara Valley Ski Resort on your right. The top of the pass, at less than 10,000 feet, comes ten miles after the town of Cuchara.

Quite a spectacular change takes place between the north side of Cucharas Pass and the south side. North- and south-facing slopes anywhere make an interesting study, but here they occur on a large scale. As you ascend the north side of the pass, notice the magnificent tall, thick stands of aspen trees. Descending the south side, evergreens and aspen yield first to ponderosa pine and scrub oak and finally to stretches of open grassland.

Within ten miles from the top of Cucharas Pass, you will encounter two lakes: the first, Trinidad North Lake, in seven miles; the second, Monument Lake, in ten. North Lake comprises a state wildlife area. Monument Lake surrounds a rock formation said to be the lithofied remains of two Indian lovers.

Highway 12 continues south to the tiny community of Stonewall. East of town at Stonewell Ranch, cattle and bison graze side by side. Today ranchers experiment with raising the two animals together. Buffalo tolerate extreme temperatures and eat some plants that cattle avoid.

Three miles beyond the ranch find New Elk Mine West. Modern coal mining bears little resemblance to early times when miners sometimes worked sixteen-hour days. In the 1890s Colorado ranked as the largest coal producer west of the Mississippi. The state could boast that its southern field contained the largest coal supply in the West.

Continue along the Purgatoire River. Spanish explorers named this river El Río de las Animas Perdidas en Purgatorio (River of the Lost Souls in Purgatory) when some of their number became lost and died without receiving the last rites. French voyageurs changed it to Purgatoire. American cowboys couldn't handle either version; they just called it Picketwire! The Purgatoire (locally pronounced Purgatory) flows from Cucharas Pass south, east and northeast to meet the Arkansas.

Drive through small Hispanic-settled towns such as Segundo and Valdez, noting the bare adobe walls on some of the buildings. Reach Cokedale Historic District and see more evidence of the once-extensive coal mining. To the right find a long line of coke ovens; to the left, hills of tailings that look like "coal dunes."

In three miles reach Trinidad State Recreation Area. Originating as an Army Corps of Engineers irrigation and flood control project, the area contains camping and picnicking spots, a lake and hiking trails. Look east from the entrance to view flat-topped Fisher's Peak standing guard over Trinidad.

Continue on Highway 12 for three miles to Trinidad. Drive under Interstate 25 and cross the Purgatoire River to the second intersection, Animas and Church Streets. See City Hall on the right and Carnegie Library on the left. Turn left at the next corner, Main Street; drive two blocks to Convent Street and turn left again. On the right find Holy Trinity Catholic Church and the Schneider Brewery, both dating from the 1880s. In one block turn right on Plum Street to the next corner, then turn right on North Commercial Street. Proceed past Church to Main, noting hotels and office blocks built both before and after 1900.

The meeting of Commercial and Main constitutes the major intersection in Trinidad. So has it been since long before the city existed; the two streets reflect converging portions of the Santa Fe Trail. At this corner rises the imposing, five-story, stone 1892 First National Bank Building, with the Jaffa Opera House across Commercial. Across Main the 1879 Columbian Hotel reflects much of Trinidad's history, having hosted lawmen (and lawless ones), dignitaries, film stars, and labor representatives. In the same block locate the Mitchell Memorial Museum and Gallery, featuring western art.

Remain on Commercial to the next street, First, and turn left. Drive one block to Maple for another left. The Las Animas County Courthouse occupies the block left of Maple along First Street.

Continue to Third Street. On your right across Third, stands the 1889 Temple Aaron, the synagogue that has been in continuous use longer than any other in Colorado. Turn left for one block and left again onto

Chestnut. Enjoy the cobblestone streets, brick sidewalks and old dwellings of Corazon de Trinidad.

Between First and Main find the Pioneer Museum. The museum fills buildings that originally housed workers hired by Don Felipe Baca, a well-to-do Hispanic rancher. At the corner of Chestnut and Main stands the Baca House, built in 1869 and oldest structure in Trinidad. Turn right on Main to view another building in the complex, the Bloom House, a majestic 1882 Victorian, once home to a merchant and banker turned cattle baron.

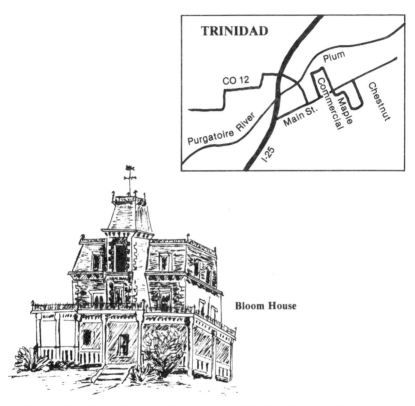

Bloom House

Turn left on Main Street, drive through Trinidad's turn-of-the-century commercial district and return to I-25. As you drive north, Greenhorn Mountain, highest peak in the Wet Mountains, dominates the view. Its name commemorates a warring Comanche chief named Green Horn or, as the Spanish called him, "Cuerno Verde," because of his massive headdress. Spanish troops under New Mexico Governor De Anza defeated the Indians in 1779.

As you cross Huerfano County line, look ahead and to the right to a cone-shaped butte. Spanish explorers titled it Huerfano (Orphan) because of its lonesome position on the plains. Continue past Walsenburg and through Pueblo to reach Colorado Springs.

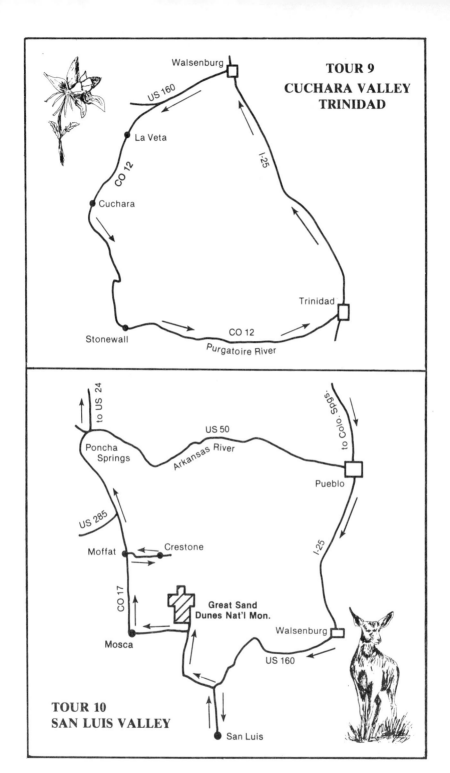

TOUR 9
CUCHARA VALLEY
TRINIDAD

Walsenburg

US 160

La Veta

CO 12

Cuchara

I-25

Trinidad

Stonewall

CO 12

Purgatoire River

to US 24

US 50

Poncha
Springs

Arkansas River

to Colo. Spgs.

Pueblo

US 285

Moffat

Crestone

I-25

CO 17

Great Sand
Dunes Nat'l Mon.

Mosca

Walsenburg

US 160

TOUR 10
SAN LUIS VALLEY

San Luis

Previous tours in this section introduce the strong Hispanic influence in Colorado's past. The San Luis Valley portion explains that history and highlights the town of San Luis, which has retained a remarkably pure cultural heritage. The tour also includes restored Fort Garland Museum and a natural masterpiece, Great Sand Dunes National Monument. You can visit the San Luis Center and the Monument all year. Fort Garland's opening spans the summer season. For a circle tour go west and north from the National Monument. This allows the delightful option of a short detour into Crestone, at the foot of the Sangre de Cristos. Continuing north from Poncha Springs puts you on the southern portion of the "Highway of the Fourteeners."

Mileage: 365 miles   *Actual driving time: 7½ hours*

As subterranean forces caused mountain building to thrust upward through existing rock layers, faults occurred. Between two faults a sink sometimes remained, visible as a high valley or meadow, often called a "park." Colorado contains North, Middle and South Parks, and the San Luis Valley. Communities with names like Woodland Park and Estes Park indicate smaller versions of the same topography.

Stretching from Poncha Pass on the north to the New Mexico state line on the south, bracketed by mountains to east and west, the five-county San Luis Valley comprises the state's largest intermontane park. Poncha Pass provides the main gateway to and from the upper Arkansas Valley. From this apex the San Juan Mountains diagonal southwest and the Sangre de Cristo Range slants southeast to enclose the valley. The Rio Grande River arrives from its westward origin, bisecting the valley as it flows into New Mexico.

Spanish involvement with the now American southwest began after a shipwreck on the east Texas coast in 1528. Only four men survived after eight years of wandering, and from one came tales of the Seven Cities of Cíbola. This myth lasted through the 1530s, until in 1540 Coronado's expedition came from Mexico on a treasure hunt. Not a golden city did they see; however, repeated explorations attested to new territory for settlement.

In 1598 Spain claimed all land in the Rio Grande drainage system and established a permanent settlement in northern New Mexico. Santa Fe followed in 1610, and until 1680 colonization continued as far north as Taos. Early in this period hunters entered the San Luis Valley, proposing to domesticate bison and take Ute slaves.

Zebulon Pike's troops built a log stockade near Sanford for winter quarters. On a subsequent foray Spanish soldiers arrested the Americans. Detained in both New and Old Mexico, Pike amassed important data before his release. He later received a brigadier general's commission in the War of 1812 and died following heroic action.

After achieving her independence, Mexico attempted to check both Indian and Anglo encroachment on her northern territory. Officials deeded enormous acreages, called land grants, with the proviso that grantees settle their holdings. The vast Sangre de Cristo Land Grant plunged into the southern San Luis Valley.

When the United States-Mexican War ended in 1848, New Mexico became American territory. With the threat of Indian reprisal controlled, residents looked north to the San Luis Valley. The first settlers arrived in 1849.

In 1852 the US Army established Fort Massachusetts six miles north of today's Fort Garland. It provided the northern anchor to a chain of forts extending along the Rio Grande from Texas. The 1850s also witnessed the founding of churches, the first flour mill, and slave traffic in Indian children. In 1858 the army exchanged Fort Massachusetts' unsatisfactory location for Fort Garland, on land leased for twenty-five years from the Sangre de Cristo Grant.

The 1860s witnessed a widening focus of interest in the San Luis Valley. Gold seekers crossed the valley to San Juan mines. The Homestead Act encouraged Anglo settlement. Toll roads over mountain passes linked the valley to other parts of the Territory.

General Palmer brought his Denver and Rio Grande over La Veta Pass. A narrow gauge vestige exists today in the Cumbres and Toltec Scenic Railroad. This branch line angled southwest before crossing the Continental Divide to reach Durango and the Silverton mines.

Another part of the valley's history deals with the Mormon colonists who arrived in the 1870s. Reaching Pueblo by train in 1877, they spent the winter on an island in the Arkansas River. The following spring they reached the San Luis Valley and selected land along the Conejos River.

Manassa, in east central Conejos County, became the Mormon colony's hub after its 1889 founding. The next year the Dempsey family arrived from Virginia. One son became the world heavyweight boxing champion, and Jack Dempsey carried a nickname, "The Manassa Mauler."

East of Manassa miners discovered turquoise deposits known to the Indians centuries ago. Near Poncha Pass miners produced gold, silver and copper. However, the mainstay of the valley remains agriculture. Famed San Luis Valley potatoes, a $100 million crop, share the spotlight with spinach, lettuce, cabbage, and carrots. Add alfalfa and the malting barley grown by Adolph Coors Company for its beer.

Begin this tour by driving south eighty-eight miles on Interstate 25 from Colorado Springs to Walsenburg. Leave the freeway at Exit 52 to reach US Highway 160 west. Follow the highway, also called "The Navajo Trail," to Fort Garland, fifty-one miles west of Walsenburg.

Turn left on Colorado Highway 159 and drive sixteen miles south to San Luis. Although not the first settlement in Colorado, others have vanished to leave San Luis the state's oldest community. Don Carlos

Beaubien founded La Plaza de San Luis de Culebra in 1851. The adobe enclave surrounded an inner plaza to provide protection. Farmers used Culebra River water to irrigate crops. The San Luis Ditch became Colorado's first water right for irrigation, priority number 1, dated 1852. At the corner of Fourth and Main Streets find the San Luis Museum, Cultural and Commercial Center on the left. Enter the gate and see a bronze plaque detailing the town's original ordinance. Note that residents had common use of pasture, wood, water, and timber. Authorities adjured citizens to keep the town clean, the roads unblocked, and to refrain from fights and quarrels as well as from drunkenness in the presence of women and children. The judge had to qualify one as a good citizen before one could buy a lot, and that lot's price reverted to the church. An old church stands across the street north of the Center.

The San Luis Center's southwestern architecture encloses a central plaza. Cross the courtyard to the museum, opened in 1980. Inside find two floors of exhibits, including a diorama of the early village, a display on how to make adobe, a Heritage Quilt by third and fourth graders, and a room styled after a morada, the Penitentes' meeting house. The Penitente lay brotherhood began in New Mexico to serve the religious community when one of the few, scattered priests could not be present.

Retrace your route toward Highway 160 and turn left into the parking lot for restored Fort Garland museum. The original Fort Garland's construction featured sun-dried adobe clay bricks, cemented with adobe mud. Squat buildings formed a rectangle around the parade ground. Whitewashed adobe finished the interiors of two barracks, officers quarters, storerooms, offices, and guardhouse.

Civil War action touched Colorado Territory when troops from Fort Garland joined militia forces at the Battle of La Glorieta Pass near Santa Fe. Sometimes called "The Gettysburg of the Southwest," Glorieta provided the North with an important victory. Confederate soldiers failed to reach Colorado's gold, the West remained in the Union, and lack of access to the Pacific Ocean assured a successful blockade of the South.

In the mid-1860s private soldiers earned $13 per month; sergeants, $17; and sergeant-majors, $23. In 1866 they all welcomed a new commander, Colonel Kit Carson. In 1868 the famed scout died, but during his brief tenure as commandant, he succeeded in pacifying the Ute Indians. Carson worked with the great Ute chief, Ouray, who even journeyed to Washington to see President Lincoln. Ute threats at the time of the Meeker Massacre in 1879 led to the strengthening of the fort. Its 1883 closing followed the removal of the Blue Sky People to a Utah reservation.

The fort land reverted to the Trinchera Estate, part of the original Sangre de Cristo Grant. In the 1920s San Luis Valley citizens organized to save the fort. In 1945 they deeded the property to the State Historical Society, and a two-year reconstruction began in 1947.

Enter today's museum and view displays that guide you through the first small building. Go outside and begin your tour of the adobe structures. Explore the commandant's quarters, reflecting Kit Carson's time. See both Carson's office and the family rooms. Next visit the former infantry barracks containing dioramas and artifacts of San Luis Valley history, stressing Indian, Hispanic and Anglo involvement.

Along the south side of the parade ground stand the buildings once used as offices, storerooms and guardhouse. Here you will find the story of "Colorado and the Civil War," emphasizing the Battle of La Glorieta Pass. On the east side the old cavalry barracks house a carriage display, a soldiers' theater and a collection of Spanish Colonial and Mexican Santos. Santos represent a unique form of American folk art. Village artisans crafted the religious statues and paintings. The Colorado Springs Fine Arts Center features one of the world's two finest Santos collections.

Leave the fort, return to Highway 160 and turn left. See Sierra Blanca Range on your right. Indians reverenced Blanca Peak, whose 14,345-foot height doubles the San Luis Valley's elevation of over 7,000 feet. Drive through the town of Blanca, an agricultural center for the valley, and continue to Colorado Highway 150. Turn right to reach Great Sand Dunes National Monument.

The arid, high-altitude valley sets the stage, and the Monument presents North America's highest dunes. Such sand piles in the American West reflect a dry climate and a supply of sand from erosion and deposition. To build the dunes requires three criteria: a large source of transportable sand, fine to medium grained; strong winds blowing in one direction; a counter wind from the opposite direction and/or a

geographical barrier. All three exist in the San Luis Valley.

Sands probably began settling in the valley with glacial streams' runoff, and the Rio Grande River added to the accumulation. Clogging sands forced the river to alter its course, leaving dry deposits in the wind's charge. Southwesterly winds blow steadily toward the Sangre de Cristos, weakening enough to drop sand at their base. Opposing winds from the northeast penetrate mountain passes to forestall any escaping sand, forcing it back into the valley.

Cycles of advancing and retreating sand also occur as Medano Creek at the dunes' edge stops advancement of, and undercuts, the hills. Sand dams the creek; the water cuts through and returns debris to the valley floor to be blown back toward the mountains once more.

Archeological evidence places man near the dunes at least 10,000 years ago. Pueblo, Navajo and Apache Indians used the valley. Utes arrived from the West. Much later came Plains Indians: Cheyenne, Arapaho, Comanche, and Kiowa.

Spanish explorers preceded Pike, Frémont and Gunnison. Captain John W. Gunnison, another army engineer, surveyed the possibility of a central transcontinental railroad from St. Louis to the Pacific.

Drive to the monument's gatehouse, pay the entry fee and continue one-half mile to the Visitors Center on the left. A nature trail and the view of the dunes' full expanse claim your attention outside; inside, enjoy displays and an informative movie.

The main dune field, within the National Monument, covers fifty square miles, stretches eight miles across, and crests at 700 feet. Daytime temperatures on the sand's surface can reach 140 degrees. Although the sand suffocates trees, both plants and animals have adapted to this inhospitable environment. Plants use long underground stems and roots to seek water and as anchors. Insects burrow, and kangaroo rats never drink water.

Leave the Visitors Center and follow the road left almost one mile to a parking lot that gives access to the dunes. A short walk takes you across the flats for a closeup view of the sand hills or a hike amid their valleys and ridges. Take time to enjoy the ripple patterns in the sand, the tenacious plants and the tracks of tiny animals. Note the S-curve, or sigmoidal ridge, that occurs at a dune's crest, dramatic visual evidence of how winds from opposite directions hit and shape the sand.

While stalking the dunes, remember the legends that arose from these awesome sand hills. One tale tells of great horses, abroad in the moonlight, running with webbed feet over the shifting sands. Other stories deal with the mysterious disappearance of a Mexican sheepherder, mules and wagons, and an orphan boy with a flock of sheep. Keep a close eye on children and personal belongings!

Leave Great San Dunes National Monument, drive eight miles south and turn right to Mosca, then turn right on Colorado Highway 17. Go north twenty-four miles to Moffat.

At Moffat you have the option of turning right to visit Crestone. The 15-minute drive allows you to view the changing ecosystems from the floor of the high mountain valley to the abruptly-rising slopes of the Sangre de Cristos, featuring Kit Carson Peak (with the flat summit) and Crestone Peak. On the way pass the Luis Maria Baca Grant; the ranch recalls a 144-square mile Spanish land grant.

Gold created Crestone, and the community now hosts a branch of the Aspen Institute. By the Baca Chalets turn left to drive through town and reach Rio Grande National Forest. Return to the Chalet sign and turn into the property. Take any road uphill to reach viewpoints that look out over the San Luis Valley to the San Juan Mountains. Also observe the small accumulations of sand that hint at how the great dunes formed. Return to Moffat to rejoin the tour.

Continue on Highway 17 for the 39-mile drive north to Poncha Springs. Notice that Poncha Pass marks the separation of watersheds, south to the Rio Grande and north to the Arkansas.

From Poncha Springs two routes provide approximately the same time and mileage to return to Colorado Springs. You may choose US Highway 50 east through Salida and Canon City to Colorado Highway 115 north. Your guide opts for the second route, north on Highway 285 to US Highway 24 east, in order to enjoy the "Highway of the Fourteeners" and view the three 14,000-foot peaks of Antero, Tabuguache and Shavano.

Colorado's Mount of the Holy Cross bears a cross formed by snow in its cracks, and Mount Shavano houses an angel. The story goes that long ago when legendary deities walked the earth, a mischievous young goddess was banished to the mountain as an angel of white ice, there to remain until some human tragedy caused her to weep. Ages passed. The angel watched the Indians come and go; she saw the settlers arrive to work the land. Then came a time of severe drought, and the angel wept for the suffering people. Her tears melted her icy limbs, and the water caused the rivers to flow once more. Now late-melting snows lodged in crevices on the mountain create the Angel of Shavano in the spring, but when summer comes she melts away to provide life-sustaining waters.

Continue to Highway 24 and drive east to Colorado Springs.

MOUNTAINS
FIVE TRIPS ON WHEELS WEST

The first thoughts any visitor to Colorado has about the state probably focus on the grandeur of the Rockies west of the Front Range cities. Colorado has the highest mean altitude of any state, over 7,000 feet. It features fifty-three peaks above 14,000 feet in elevation. Among the major rivers that rise in the mountain heights number the Platte and Arkansas flowing east, the Rio Grande heading south and the Colorado moving west.

Many of the prime features of Colorado history also center on the high country. Ute Indians inhabited the mountain land for hundreds of years. Fur trappers brought out fortunes in pelts. The Rush to the Rockies for mineral treasures yielded unbelievable bonanzas in gold and silver. Seemingly impossible mountain railroad building required skill, ingenuity and perseverance to try the hardiest entrepreneur. For modern adventurers Colorado's dry powder snow provides some of the world's finest skiing.

Take a trip to the tundra in Rocky Mountain National Park. Follow the mining mystique to towns such as Aspen, Black Hawk, Central City, Georgetown, Silver Plume, Breckenridge, and Fairplay. Add Leadville, once the world's richest silver source, and Cripple Creek, once the world's greatest gold camp. Enjoy the historic resort communities of Estes Park, Grand Lake, Glenwood Springs, and Manitou Springs.

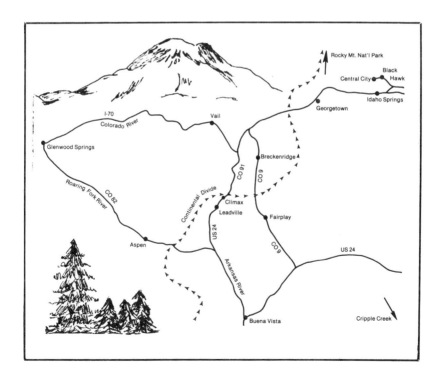

87

ROCKY MOUNTAIN NATIONAL PARK

Coming to Colorado and not seeing Rocky Mountain National Park is like coming to Colorado Springs and not seeing the Air Force Academy Chapel. The former ranks as the state's most popular natural attraction; the latter as the biggest drawing card among man-made destinations. On a one-day jaunt allow at least three hours in the park. For extra enjoyment make binoculars part of your equipment.

Trail Ridge Road remains open from approximately Memorial Day until mid-October. However, even during this limited season the road may close temporarily due to storms. Although you cannot cross the park all year, portions at both sides remain accessible. To the east find Hidden Valley ski area. To the west, Trail Ridge serves as a snowmobile course from the Grand Lake entrance to Poudre Lake, weather permitting. Also, the Visitors Centers at Park Headquarters and at Grand Lake remain open.

Both Estes Park and Grand Lake welcome visitors at any time of year. When Trail Ridge closes, reverse the tour's return route and reach Grand Lake by Highways 40 and 34.

Mileage: 350 miles   *Actual driving time: 7½ hours*

The word "park" in place names like Estes Park and Woodland Park refers to a high meadow and valley region below the mountain peaks. Joel Estes picked this park for settlement after seeing it in 1859.

Estes Park developed in the 1870s when homesteading, tourism and land speculation arrived. Ranchers came to homestead and raise cattle. Tourists sought both outdoor pursuits and good health, finding room and board for as little as eight dollars per week. Windham Thomas Wyndham-Quinn, fourth Earl of Dunraven, Irish aristocrat and avid hunter, tried to buy up land and drive out the settlers. Although he purchased over 6,000 acres and built a hunting lodge and a hotel, other residents successfully contested his monopoly.

Miss Isabella Lucy Bird, a diminutive Victorian gentlewoman in her forties, remains a memorable visitor. Daughter of an Anglican cleric, she abandoned her sickbed to roam the globe. She learned to ride a horse astride, rather than sidesaddle, while visiting Hawaii and donned Hawaiian riding togs. Enthusiastic reports then led her to Colorado Territory; her destination became Estes Park after a Dunraven associate extolled its beauty. Isabella finally reached Estes, met "Rocky Mountain Jim" Nugent, climbed Longs Peak, rode her beloved pony on a round-trip trek from Estes to Colorado Springs, and saw her letters to her sister become a book called *A Lady's Life in the Rocky Mountains*.

Jim Nugent built his cabin at the entrance to Estes and appointed himself the park's guardian. Despite a restless temper, ragged clothes and a face disfigured on one side from a grizzly bear attack, Jim once was a handsome, cultured gentleman. He and Isabella Bird developed a mutual attraction, but they realized its incongruity and parted friends. Before his death from a wound inflicted by a Dunraven supporter, Jim penned the following invective to the *Fort Collins Standard:* "Is this your boasted Colorado? That I, an American citizen who had trod upon Colorado's soil since '54 must have my life attempted ... for British gold!"

Rocky Mountain became the tenth national park to be set aside for the preservation and protection of our natural heritage. Around 1900 conservationist, writer and naturalist Enos Mills and his colleagues began a crusade to create the park. Established in 1915, the park covers over four hundred square miles. Its acreage straddles the Continental Divide and boasts twenty peaks over 13,000 feet. On its eastern edge Longs Peak stands 14,256 feet high. Across the Divide near the park's north boundary rises the North Fork of the Colorado River.

The unique ecological experience of a simulated journey to the Arctic rates among the most important aspects of Rocky Mountain National Park. Traversing the windswept highlands above treeline puts you in the Arctic-Alpine life zone where you will see plants normally found as far north as Alaska. The alpine tundra closely resembles its Arctic cousin although the mountain heights do not duplicate the far north's summer of light and winter of darkness. In each case no trees grow and plants stay small, compact and close to the ground to survive the elemental struggle with wind and cold.

Trail Ridge Road spans Rocky Mountain National Park for a distance of some forty miles. During the construction period of 1929-1932, the work crew of 150 men took extraordinary precautions to preserve the park's ecology. Parts of the road echo an old trail used by both Ute and Arapaho Indians. Along the drive twelve arrowhead markers indicate points of interest. Trail Ridge reaches an altitude of 12,183 feet to become the highest through road in North America. Others, like the roads up Mount Evans and Pikes Peak, climb higher but deadend at the summit.

Grand Lake constitutes Colorado's largest natural body of water. Glaciers hollowed out the deep depression, then left piles of rock called moraines to act as a dam. Many man-made lakes, including its neighbors, Shadow Mountain and Granby, now surpass Grand Lake in size.

Historically, the first humans to reach Grand Lake's shores were Ute Indians; later came the Cheyenne and Arapaho. They all enjoyed summering in this land rich with game and fish. However, the Utes in their mountain homeland became bitter enemies of the encroaching Plains tribes. Legend has it that during a bloody battle, Ute braves used rafts on the lake to carry their women and children out of danger. Safety eluded them, however, when heavy winds blew the rafts far from shore and caused them to capsize. All passengers drowned, and the few surviving braves forsook the lake. Grand Lake bears a second name, Spirit Lake, since the early morning mists and echoes are said to be spirits of the Ute women and children.

French fur trappers penetrated the area and named "le grand lac." In 1853 after John C. Frémont's exploration, the anglicized form, Grand Lake, appeared. The first permanent white settler, Civil War veteran Joseph L. Wescott, arrived in 1867. After the grizzly mauled Jim Nugent, Mountain Jim struggled to the pioneer's cabin, and Wescott nursed him back to health.

A brief boom hit in the 1880s when traces of gold showed up to the north. Wescott saw his private fishing hole become a supply center for mining hopefuls.

The Grand Lake Yacht Club began in 1902 and enjoys the distinction of being the highest registered yacht club in the world. Regatta Week, featuring the Lipton Cup Race, occurs every summer. Tea company founder Thomas Lipton presented the first Lipton Cup in 1912.

Dubbed "The Playground of the Rockies," Grand and its sister lakes, Shadow Mountain and Granby, feature angling for trout, salmon and pike. Village visitors enjoy summer stock theater and Western Week with a buffalo barbeque. You can ride boats, horses or "klunkers" (low-maintenance bicycles that handle four-wheel-drive roads). Winter sports include cross-country skiing, snowshoeing and ice fishing, but snowmobiling takes the spotlight. Shadow Mountain Lake provides the course for the annual Colorado Snowmobiling Championships.

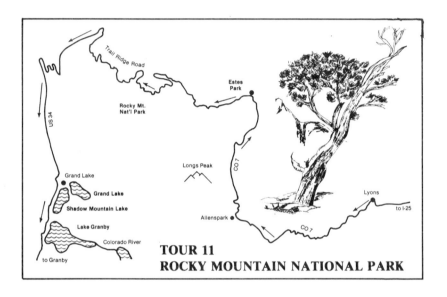

TOUR 11
ROCKY MOUNTAIN NATIONAL PARK

Begin this tour by driving north on Interstate 25 through Denver to Exit 243. Turn west on Colorado Highway 66, following the signs for Lyons, Estes Park and Rocky Mountain National Park.

As you drive north of Denver and west toward Lyons, notice the rich farming lands of Weld County, one of the largest agricultural producers in the United States. Early attempts at irrigation testified to the fact that the Eastern Slope provided the fertile acreage, but the Western Slope retained the water. Just as the Fryingpan-Arkansas diversion irrigates the Arkansas Valley so also does the Colorado-Big Thompson Project water the plains north of Denver.

Drive into Lyons. At the junction of US Highway 36 and Colorado Highway 7, turn left onto 7. Move from creek and canyon into national forest land. Drive north along the eastern boundary of Rocky Mountain

National Park, close to the base of Longs Peak, and pass the Enos Mills Homestead.

As you near Estes Park, look ahead to Lakes Estes, second of six reservoirs east of the Continental Divide designed to hold water from the Colorado and Big Thompson Rivers. Across from the lake stands a small historic museum. An aerial tram reveals views of Longs Peak, the Continental Divide and Rocky Mountain National Park.

Drive to Highway 36 and turn left. Continue to the junction of Highways 36 and 34. Drive straight ahead on 34 west and go right at the first turn to visit the Stanley Hotel, listed on the National Register of Historic Places.

When Lord Dunraven had to sell some of his holdings, one of the buyers was F. O. Stanley, manufacturer of the Stanley Steamer automobile. Stanley, a consumptive, came to Estes in 1903 with his doctor's prediction of only months to live. He experienced the Rocky Mountain cure, finally dying at age 91 in 1946, having become beloved as Estes Park's benefactor. In 1909 his lavish Stanley Hotel opened eighty-eight guestrooms. A fleet of thirteen Steamers made the trip to Lyons twice a day to meet incoming train passengers.

Visit the Stanley, return to Highway 36 and continue through Estes Park. Note the Courtyard Shops to the right and the colorful array of businesses along the main street. Turn left on Moraine Avenue to reach the toll gate into Rocky Mountain National Park. Stop at headquarters for information and slide programs.

Leave the Visitors Center and proceed into the park, enjoying a panoramic view of Longs Peak to the left. The peak carries the name of U.S. Army topographic engineer and explorer Stephen H. Long and stands fifteenth tallest of Colorado's "fourteeners." In 1864 Editor William Byers of Denver's *Rocky Mountain News* predicted that "no living creature unless it had wings" would climb Longs Peak. However, Byers himself, as a member of John Wesley Powell's party, achieved the first ascent in 1868.

Drive to Deer Creek Junction where Trail Ridge Road starts. As you begin the ascent, watch for the arrowhead markers and use the road guide to identify and enjoy the designated stopping places. Pause at overlooks where birds like the saucy, gray Clark's nutcrackers and blue, black-crested Stellar's jays join chipmunks and ground squirrels in a bid for attention.

Throughout your visit to the park observe results of glacial activity. Glaciers, often described as "rivers of ice," produce changes to the landscape as they flow along the bedrock surface. Most glaciation processes involve either erosion, the removal of rock material; or deposition, the unloading or dropping of material. Use this "glossary of glaciation" to spot ice-caused features.

U-shaped valley	— *in contrast to stream-cut, V-shaped valleys, valleys cut by glacial ice masses look more U-shaped*
cirque	— *large bowl formed high on the side of a glacial valley appearing to form a giant amphitheater*
arete	— *single, jagged, crested ridge between the sidewalls of two cirques*
moraine	— *accumulated debris laid down beneath, at the side of, or at the end of a glacier*

As you climb to over 12,000 feet, notice stands of aspen, pine, juniper, fir, and spruce trees. After passing Rainbow Curve (Sign 4), look to the left at the stripped tree skeletons that bear mute testimony to harsh extremes of climate. Elsewhere along the road find wind-battered trees whose branches grow only to one side, giving them the name "flag trees." Pass the last weatherbeaten trees to reach timberline and the fragile, exposed world of the tundra.

Severe weather conditions—summer drought and thunderstorms, winter blizzards and violent wind—create a rigorous climate in which only specially adapted plants and animals survive. Look for the scuttling, furry marmot and marvel at the dainty high alpine flowers (often termed "belly flowers" for the level at which you find the best view). The alpine tundra world of Rocky Mountain National Park features a very brief growing season of no more than twelve weeks. Annual plants demonstrate a speeded-up yearly growth cycle; perennials may take several hundred years to mature.

Trail Ridge Road crests at 12,183 feet after the Lava Cliffs (Sign 7). Alpine Visitors Center contains tundra displays and park information, with schedules of programs and naturalist-guided hikes. Although you have passed the road's highest point, the Continental Divide lies ahead at Milner Pass.

At Farview Curve (Sign 11) on the Divide's west side view the North Fork of the Colorado River flowing through Kawuneeche Valley. Continue to the end of Trail Ridge Road and the Grand Lake Entrance to Rocky Mountain National Park. Exit the park and drive two miles on Highway 34 to its junction with Colorado Highway 278.

Turn left on Highway 278 to Grand Lake, the village, and Grand Lake, the lake. At the Y take the left road, marked Big Thompson Irrigation Tunnel. In one mile cross a bridge and note a dirt road going downhill to the right. This is where you will turn when you come back from the tunnel. In another mile reach the east end of the lake by an information board explaining how the Colorado-Big Thompson water diversion project utilizes reservoirs and power plants on both sides of the Continental Divide and sends water through the 13-mile tunnel to eastern slope farmland.

Retrace your route for 1.2 miles and turn left before the bridge. At the bottom of the hill turn right over a second bridge to reach the village of

Grand Lake. The picturesque little community features an Old West look with wooden sidewalks.

Leave Grand Lake heading south on Highway 34. Pass Shadow Mountain Lake; note the "ski area" sign on the right and turn left at the sign for the Granby Pumping Plant. The plant reaches twelve stories below and four above ground level. One of its three huge pumps can pump enough water in two minutes to supply an individual's lifetime needs.

In addition to altering the landscape by creating Shadow Mountain and Granby Lakes, the Big Thompson project also changed the source of the Colorado River. Once originating in Grand Lake, the Colorado now begins at Granby Dam on its 1,400 mile course, along the way forming the Grand Canyon and irrigating California agriculture.

Return to Highway 34, turn left and continue to US Highway 40. Turn left and drive through Middle Park territory and the town of Granby. Pass through Fraser, billing itself as "the icebox of the nation," since it historically has posted some of the United States' lowest temperatures.

Reach Winter Park, a ski resort administered as one of Denver's mountain parks. Shortly after the turn of the century veteran railroad man David Moffat's Denver, Northwestern and Pacific line labored over the Continental Divide at 11,600 feet. Officials expected this blizzard-battered, steep-graded Rollins Pass route to serve as a temporary line until a tunnel bored through the mountains. Twenty-four years later the Moffat Tunnel cut the rail distance to Salt Lake City and put Denver on a transcontinental railroad for the first time. In 1928 people began taking the train to ski the old logging roads near the tunnel's west portal.

Continue on Highway 40 up Berthoud Pass to cross the Continental Divide. In 1861 Denver businessmen agreed upon the need for a stage and wagon road from the Mile High City through Middle Park to Salt Lake City and California. Young engineer E. L. Berthoud won the "pathfinding" job of locating a feasible route. Berthoud's experience included building a railroad across Panama, and his exploration party featured famed mountain man Jim Bridger. Berthoud left the mining town of Empire one morning in May and the following day followed a creek to the pass that bears his name. Fourteen years elapsed before the stagecoach from Georgetown crossed Berthoud Pass to Fraser's site.

Berthoud Pass has a history of avalanche problems. As you descend its east side, pick out tracks down the mountain where flattened trees tell the story. Aspen fill in the devastated areas first, and evergreens finally take over again. Also look to the left as you go downhill to see the evidence of glacial activities—a large cirque, topped by an arete.

Note the sign for the Henderson Mine. You may wish to detour three and one-half miles to this AMAX molybdenum property. The Henderson orebody, 300 million tons of moly, represents one of the world's largest deposits. Moly's primary use is to make steel more versatile, tough and resistant. A small Visitors Center explains the mine and the moly.

Reach Empire, where Colorado's general mining craze hit in 1860. Ute Indians followed a trail over Berthoud Pass and stopped in Empire on the way to Denver for trading. Supplies of wild hay from Middle Park meadows reached the town by the same route.

Pass through Empire to reach Interstate 70 east. Exit I-70 at Sixth Avenue, continue east to Interstate 25 and turn south to Colorado Springs.

ASPEN — GLENWOOD SPRINGS

Scoffers will say, "You can't make this drive in one day!" But if that's all the time you have, you certainly can. Try a long summer day, get an early start, and budget the number and duration of your stops.

In addition to the autumn colors, early fall also makes a lovely time to tour because you miss both the summer and the winter throngs. A fond memory recalls visiting an Aspen watering hole in the off season and encountering a large dog perched on a bar stool, looking for all the world as though he were about to order a drink. And that, come to think of it, says a great deal about the Aspen ambience!

You don't have to be a skier to enjoy winter in the mountains. Aspen hosts a winter carnival in January. And what could be nicer than a cold day outdoors followed by a soak in Glenwood's hot pool?

Although this is a trip for any season, Independence Pass does not stay open all year. Its schedule depends upon the weather; we've seen it open at Christmas and closed the first week in June. Reach Aspen via Glenwood when the pass closes.

Mileage: 480 miles   *Actual driving time: 9½ hours*

One of Colorado's most magical names, Aspen, calls forth memories of a silver boom in the mining days and dreams of pristine white powder snow on today's ski slopes. Aspen also headquarters nationally and internationally recognized summer programs in the arts and humanities.

Credit for beginning a permanent town by the Roaring Fork River goes to thirteen stalwart settlers who braved one of Colorado's worst winters to remain in the mountain-rimmed valley. Their fellow adventurers retreated to Leadville following news of the Meeker Massacre. Ute Indians, rebelling at continued encroachment upon their land, killed Agent Nathan Meeker and eleven other men at the White River Indian Agency and kidnapped women and children.

The following year, 1880, saw the platting of Aspen and regular mule train service over the difficult Continental Divide route to Leadville delivering ore to smelters. Aspen silver mining enjoyed bonanza status for the next thirteen years. The Smuggler Mine produced the world's largest silver nugget, weighing roughly one ton. Aspen became the largest Colorado city west of the Divide, the major business center between Denver and Salt Lake City, and the first community in the state to have electric lights.

Jerome Wheeler, of Macy's in New York, arrived in 1883 and involved himself in a variety of commercial enterprises, including ranching, mining, smelting, quarrying, banking, railroading, and adding the Hotel Jerome and the Wheeler Opera House to the Aspen scene.

Toasted as the "Crystal City of the Rockies," Aspen saw its population plummet after 1893's demonitization of silver. However, the spectacular mountain scenery and the snow's white gold presaged a twentieth century recovery. The 1932 Olympics at Lake Placid turned U.S. eyes toward ski resorts. Andre Roch of Switzerland — skier, mountaineer, engineer, avalanche expert — looked over Aspen Mountain and acclaimed its powder snow as better than anything in Europe. He designed Roch Run racing trail, and a first race in 1939 preceded the 1941 National Alpine Championships.

World War II brought the elite Tenth Mountain Division to train at Camp Hale and to spend leave time in Aspen, where the Hotel Jerome rented them rooms for fifty cents a night. In 1945 war veteran and Austrian ski champion Friedl Pfeifer returned to assist Chicago industrialist Walter Paepcke in fostering the renaissance of Aspen. Paepcke, head of the Container Corporation of America, envisioned a center where arts and ideas would co-exist with a healthy physical program. In 1949 the first Aspen Institute for Humanistic Studies welcomed Dr. Albert Schweitzer as its honored guest, and Artur Rubenstein helped the Aspen Music Festival begin its acclaimed career.

Meanwhile back on the slopes, efforts matured in January 1947. The town witnessed its official opening as a winter resort, with Pfeifer heading the ski school, and the christening of the world's longest chair lift. World championships tested the mountain in 1950.

Interesting personalities have permeated the Aspen scene since silver mining days. Lillian Russell and John Drew played the Wheeler Opera House. Damon Runyon served as a bellhop at the Hotel Jerome. Editor Harold Ross, who founded *The New Yorker* magazine, grew up in Aspen. Architect Eero Saarinen designed the Music Tent. The list of luminaries associated with summer programs goes on indefinitely.

At the confluence of the Colorado and the Roaring Fork, two river valleys join in one of the Ute Indians' oldest hunting and meeting places. Indians called the hot springs that bubble from under the earth "Yampah" (Big Medicine) and considered them sacred, coming yearly for ritual bathing.

As Leadville and Aspen silver mining fortunes grew, the bonanza kings looked for a non-mining playground in which to invest time and money. Glenwood Springs, like Colorado Springs, developed in an atmosphere of refinement, wealth and culture.

Jerome Wheeler employed a young mining engineer, Walter Devereux, who made a silver fortune in his own right. James J. Hagerman of the Colorado Midland joined Devereux and his brothers in encouraging English capitalists to partner Western gold and silver magnates in Glenwood Springs investments.

The year of 1887 brought a variety of disparate events. Famous old Ute Chief Colorow attempted a futile last stand before his death the following year. Infamous gambler and gunman Doc Holliday died in bed of TB and lies buried on Cemetery Hill. The Devereux brothers purchased Yampah Hot Springs for $125,000 and added ten acres on the Roaring Fork for a race track and polo field.

Under Devereux ownership the hot waters serviced both Natatorium and Inhalatorium. The bathhouse (the current Hot Springs Lodge) included Roman baths and a casino where the proper dress featured white tie and tails. The Inhalatorium provided thick, foggy steam, and in the vapor caves clients sat lined up on marble benches encased in heavy linen bags like mummies.

When one had bathed, breathed and perspired one's way to better health and a beautiful complexion, there remained such pursuits as outdoor sports, railway excursions and life in the grand manner. With all the amenities but no competition, promoters taught local cowboys how to play polo and found that both they and their ponies made top competitors. Glenwood's polo team won the world championship in 1903, 1904 and 1912.

The D&RG and the Midland sought to outdo each other in special train offerings. In addition to Saturday nights' "laundry trains" or "bath trains" from Leadville and Aspen, railroads hauled crowds to social and sporting events: to Sunday School picnics and fishing, to circuses, and to view bicycle races from Glenwood to Basalt.

To complete the picture, one of Colorado's great hotels had its grand opening in 1893. Designed in sixteenth-century Italian style after the Villa Medici, the Hotel Colorado aspired to a top position among state hotels, second only to Denver's Brown Palace. Within the $850,000 brick and sandstone edifice, two hundred rooms welcomed wealthy and titled guests. Modern restoration of the hotel restores its former elegance.

Begin this tour by driving west on US Highway 24 for 115 miles through Buena Vista to Colorado Highway 82. Turn left for eighteen miles to the summit of Independence Pass.

Ascending Colorado's altitudes one visits five of the six life zones in North America, experiencing the ecology of latitudes from Mexico to Alaska. Going up Independence you pass treeline and reach an alpine tundra environment at its 12,095-foot crest. Short trails at the summit allow you to explore this land high above sea level.

Descend Independence Pass on its west side, passing the old ghost town of Independence on the left. Reach Aspen city limits and continue across the Roaring Fork River into town. Follow Highway 82 to Main Street.

Using the Hotel Jerome at Main and Mill Streets as a reference point, find many shops and restaurants across Main Street toward Aspen Mountain. Behind the Jerome locate Hallam Lake Nature Preserve, blocks of Victorian houses, and the facilities of Aspen Music Festival and Aspen Institute. Turn right on Mill to find free parking.

Walk on Mill across Main and two blocks toward Aspen Mountain. At the corner of Mill and Hyman stands the Wheeler Opera House. From its 1889 beginning through its 1984 remodeling, the three-story brick building has been an Aspen landmark. In festive mining days performers played "The Silver Circuit." In 1984 two years of extensive renovation culminated in a gala reopening. Actress Lillian Gish, whose return to an old mining town recalled her early appearance at the Central City Opera House, helped launch the restored hall.

Across the street from the Opera House lies Wagner Park on the right; straight ahead and left, the pedestrian mall. On Mill and to your left, filling the mall and streets beyond, locate blocks ready for shopping and browsing, eating and drinking. Brick sidewalks, benches, trees, flowers, and running water complete the mall.

Return to your car and drive on Mill away from the ski slopes. Three blocks from Main turn left on Puppy Smith Street, pass the post office and reach a deadend at the Nature Preserve. Walk down the path to Hallam Lake. This 22-acre center shelters wildlife close to town and also recalls that the lake once provided ice for the community and featured amusement park, dance pavilion and boardwalk.

Retrace your route along Puppy Smith Street to Mill and turn right. Turn right again on Bleeker Street, one block before Main. Drive two blocks to Aspen Street, then begin a series of stairstep turns right and left along streets of Victorian homes to Lake Avenue: turn right on Aspen, left on Hallam, right on Garmisch, left on Francis, right on First, and make a little jog left on Smuggler to a right at Lake. Surrounding the small triangular park bordered by Lake, Smuggler and Second stands a wealth of dwellings typical of Aspen's silver days.

Drive two blocks on Lake to a left onto Gillespie. Park as indicated and walk into the meadow to see the Music Tent and visit Aspen Institute. Enter the Institute to view gallery space and note a long wall sculpture detailing people and ideas that have influenced studies past and present. Walk through the outdoor courtyard to a small park in the mountain meadow.

Return to your car and continue on Gillespie until you must turn left at Sixth. Note the Physics Institute on your right. Continue four streets to Hallam and turn right to pick up Highway 82 out of town.

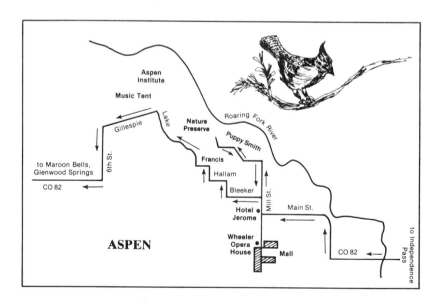

Drive less than one mile and turn left to the alpinesque Aspen Chapel. Take the right fork, Maroon Creek Road, leading to Maroon Lake and Maroon Bells, one of the most photographed vistas in the country. During the summer months you must take a shuttle bus from Aspen Highlands; otherwise, you may drive up the valley of Maroon Creek to the lake and the Bells, two rugged, glaciated peaks.

Retrace your route to Highway 82 and turn left. Follow the stream to the little town of Basalt where the Roaring Fork and the Fryingpan Rivers meet and continue by Mount Sopris into Glenwood Springs, thirty-eight miles from Aspen. In Glenwood the highway becomes Grand Avenue.

Continue on Grand over the bridge crossing the Colorado River. Turn right at the traffic light just across the bridge to view Hotel Colorado, the pools and the entrance to the vapor caves. Across the river see the old Denver and Rio Grande depot.

If you have time for a swim, return to the traffic light by the bridge and continue straight ahead, following the signs to Interstate 70. Turn left, noting the Interstate directly in front of you, and turn left immediately on North River Street. Park as space permits. Continue past the Hot Springs Lodge, site of the Devereux Roman baths and casino, to the entrance of "the world's largest natural warm mineral water open air pool."

Enterprising Walter Devereux diverted the Colorado River to reveal the source of the hot springs from which flow daily 3.5 million gallons of 124- to 130-degree water. The large pool extends 405 feet (about two blocks) in length and up to 100 feet in width. It holds over a million gallons of water. Regulation of temperature keeps the water between 86 and 89 degrees in the summer and 90 degrees during the winter. At one hundred feet, the small therapy pool is as long as the large pool is wide. The hot pool's temperature holds at 102 to 104 degrees all year. Whirlpools in the small pool and a water slide at the end of the large pool provide further aquatic enjoyment.

Exit Glenwood via I-70 eastbound and enter Glenwood Canyon. Here the Colorado River has cut a majestic swath through the rocky cliffs. Pass Shoshone Hydroelectric Plant. Completed in 1909, this represents the first damming of the Colorado River's westward flow.

Pass the towns of Gypsum and Eagle. Fifty miles from Glenwood reach Avon. On the hillside note the ski slopes and baronial dwellings at Beaver Creek, home of former president Gerald Ford.

Drive ten more miles to reach Vail. Ute Indians enjoyed this valley as a summer home. British nobleman Lord Gore led the first white settlers here in 1880. Still unspoiled in the early 1960s, the Gore Valley saw the boom begin in 1963, and now buildings associated with Vail stretch for miles along the highway on each side and in both directions.

To balance the business brought by winter snows, state ski areas have

Maroon Bells

begun summer programs in global affairs, sports and the arts. In 1982 President Ford conceived the World Forum for international government and corporate leaders to meet and discuss world trade. Also under the Ford aegis occur the annual Jerry Ford Invitational Golf Tournament and the Jerry Ford Celebrity Ski Race.

Leave Vail, one hundred miles west of Denver, and climb Vail Pass. Note the paved bike path between the eastbound and westbound lanes of the Interstate.

You are in Coors International Bicycle Classic country. A pre-Olympic race in 1984 marked the tenth anniversary of a marathon that gives real meaning to the word "grueling." Riders amass a winning time total by competing in a nine-day series of races, including pedaling over 11,992-foot Loveland Pass, on sections in Eastern Slope cities, and west to Grand Junction. In the special pre-Olympic event men covered almost 670 miles; women, about 270.

Start up the Continental Divide to the 11,158-foot elevation of the Eisenhower-Edwin C. Johnson Memorial Tunnel which takes you through, rather than over, the summit. Dwight D. Eisenhower, whose wife, Mamie, came from Denver, maintained close ties with Colorado during his presidency. "Big Ed" Johnson served as the state's governor and United States Senator during the 1930s, 40s, and 50s.

Drive down the east side of the Divide and pass Silver Plume, Georgetown and Idaho Springs. Continue to Denver, taking Sixth Avenue exit to meet Interstate 25 south to Colorado Springs.

WHERE THE MINES WERE

It sounds appalling to contemplate a day's tour that includes nine different towns; you could spend a whole day in just one or two of them! However, some, like Black Hawk, Silver Plume and Alma are very small and can be viewed in a short time. Others, like Golden and Idaho Springs reveal many points of interest even if you only drive through them.

Your guide suggests stopping at Central City, Georgetown and Breckenridge, and reserving a little time at the end for Fairplay. The distance from Black Hawk to Fairplay is less than one hundred miles, and you can cover it in two hours.

Don't think this is just a summer trip. We made one research journey on December 19. The towns looked like Christmas cards; the roads were clear and the mountains magnificent. With minimal stops, we reached home before dark.

Mileage: 275 miles   *Actual driving time: 6 hours*

The California gold rush of 1849 preceded by ten years the profitable discovery of gold in Colorado's mountains. Many successful prospectors in the Rockies cut their mining teeth in the California boom and brought to Colorado their experience in locating and extracing the precious metal. The false start at Denver's Cherry Creek in 1858 gave way to valuable claims in 1859, and Colorado mining was in business—very big business. Like a precocious child, the Colorado bonanza surpassed its California forerunner many times over; success begat success as the mountains yielded not only gold but also silver and less exotic minerals.

Extraction methods ranged from placer washing to hard rock blasting. Mechanization arrived early with simple implements such as the rocker, the sluice box and the Long Tom. Similar to, but an improvement upon, the panning technique, each used flushing and/or shaking to eventually separate gold from gravel. Ore-bearing lodes tantalized miners near the surface, but the true wealth hid underground and required blasting, tunnels, timbers for shoring up diggings, hoists, and, finally, crushers and mills to refine the ore.

Three brothers from Georgia, the Russells, found Colorado's first placer gold in 1858, but credit for beginning the real rush in 1859 goes to John Gregory, also a Georgian. The plan of rules for the Gregory Mining District in the Central City-Black Hawk area predated all others in the Territory. The first to be recorded, it served as a basis for future Colorado mining law.

Founders of many Colorado towns that sprang up as a result of the 1859 boom glorified their frontier existence by appending "City" to settlement names. Golden City lay up Clear Creek Canyon west of Denver City and Auraria, closer to Gregory's Diggings.

A popular Golden City hobby in the early days involved flinging challenges at Denver: to be territorial capital, to control the supply traffic to the mines, to locate the major railroad terminus. After Colorado City's short-lived role as territorial capital, Golden successfully took the title for several years in the 1860s; however, Denver eventually fought off that challenge. The Mile High City also scored as the principal supply depot. Golden's William A. H. Loveland joined Edward L. Berthoud to begin the Colorado Central Railroad, planning to connect with Union Pacific tracks in Wyoming, but Denver Pacific promoters met this threat by running a line to Cheyenne.

The drive from Golden through Clear Creek Canyon leads to the site of Gregory's original diggings and the adjacent towns of Black Hawk and Central City. The two towns began as mining rivals but each established its own identity. Central became known as "the richest square mile on earth" and "The Little Kingdom of Gilpin" (for Gilpin County); Black Hawk developed as a city of mills.

First came simple stamp mills whose operators raised heavy weights, then dropped them to crush the ore. As mining continued deeper into the earth, however, the gold ore appeared in combination with other elements, and more sophisticated techniques became necessary. Boston investors retained Nathaniel P. Hill, chemistry professor from Brown University, to assess their mine holdings. He solved the problem of smelting Colorado ores. Twice Hill traveled to Wales, shipping Little Kingdom ores for reduction. His research and observations resulted in the 1867 organization of the Boston and Colorado Smelting Company at Black Hawk. The Colorado Central Railroad pushed through in 1872, and the Little Kingdom had facilities for the full mining process: extraction, reduction and transportation.

Despite the fame attached to Gregory's Diggings, George Jackson was the original Fifty-Niner. In January 1859 he managed to scratch out a small quantity of gold from the frozen ground near Clear Creek in sight of some steaming hot springs. Jackson spent the winter in Denver and returned in the spring to both placer and lode mining. Jackson's Diggings became the town of Idaho Springs.

In the 1870s two events widened Idaho Springs' appeal. The hot springs gained fame for their curative value, and an industry developed to bottle and ship the water. The railroad also arrived, and tourists came into the mountains even as ore traveled out of them.

Kentuckian George Griffith founded the Griffith Mining District with George's Town as its headquarters. Miners began to move on as the gold supply failed to satisfy all comers, but 1864 brought discoveries of silver. Georgetown realized its fame as "The Silver Queen of the Rockies." Unlike most prospecting settlements, Georgetown never suffered a major fire and boasts over two hundred original buildings.

Even such a formidable barrier as the Continental Divide did not deter gold seekers. Across the Divide from Georgetown and Silver Plume in the valley of the Blue River, placer discoveries led to the founding of Breckenridge in 1859. Within a few years the familiar story of easy-come, easy-go placer mining followed, and many prospectors left for new strikes or for the Civil War. A second boom came in the late 1870s with lode mining. In 1887 two miners at the Gold Flake Mine dug out Colorado's largest gold nugget — thirteen pounds, seven ounces Troy — known as "Tom's Baby," after one of its founders.

Not until the turn of the century did the unique dredge boats appear on the Breckenridge scene to write another chapter in Colorado mining history. Flat-bottomed 50-foot boats took to the Blue River carrying dredging machinery to the gold. Dredges scooped up buckets of gold-bearing sand and gravel, washed and separated out the ore and spewed forth mountains of rejected rocks. As the equipment dredged up the stream beds, the supposedly played-out placer deposits came to life once more, producing until the 1940s. Even today ecologically-conscious dredging occurs on the Arkansas River.

Hoosier Pass crosses the Continental Divide between Breckenridge and the small communities of Alma and Fairplay on the Eastern Slope. Products of the Pikes Peak or Bust boom, the towns later sent both freighters' wagons and stagecoaches over 13,000-foot Mosquito Pass to Leadville.

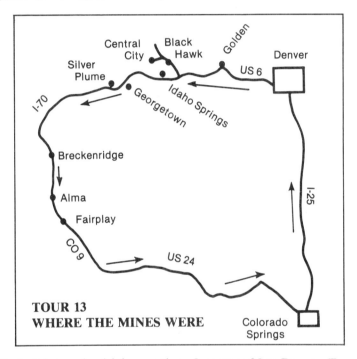

TOUR 13
WHERE THE MINES WERE

Begin this tour by driving north on Interstate 25 to Denver. Turn west on Sixth Avenue (US Highway 6) to Golden, some eighty miles from Colorado Springs. Turn right off Highway 6 at Nineteenth to enter Golden, territorial capital from 1862 until 1867.

To view Colorado School of Mines, second only to Colorado College as the Rockies' pioneer higher educational institution, turn left at the first street, Elm, drive one block and turn right, following the curve to Maple. Find Mines' Geology Museum, featuring important and historic mineral collections, on the right at Maple and Sixteenth. Continue to Thirteenth, turn right, drive one block, and turn right again. Note Simon Guggenheim Hall (Old Main) on the right at Fifteenth; the Guggenheim fortune began with Colorado mining connections.

Drive to Eighteenth, turn left three blocks to Washington and turn left again. Washington is Golden's main street; follow it to Thirteenth and turn right three blocks to Coors parking lot.

In 1873 Adolph Coors and Jacob Schueler founded a brewery in Golden. Coors bought out his partner in 1880, and Adolph Coors Company has been a family business ever since. In addition to the brewery, Coors Industries has diversified into some twenty subsidiaries, including Coors Procelain, Coors Food Products, Coors Energy, and Coors Transportation. Shuttle buses take visitors to the hospitality center for a tour of the brewery and a free sample.

Leave the Coors parking lot, cross Washington and turn right on the next street, Arapahoe, for one block. Look left at Thirteenth and Arapahoe to view the old Armory. Wagons brought rocks from Clear Creek Canyon to create the largest cobblestone building in the country. Turn right on Twelfth to pass the 1867 Astor House, first stone hotel west of St. Louis.

Turn left on Washington, cross Clear Creek and proceed to Colorado Highway 58. Turn left, drive to Highway 6 and go right. Drive west through Clear Creek Canyon, following the Colorado Central railroad route to Gregory's Diggings.

After eleven miles reach Colorado Highway 119 and turn right toward Central City and Black Hawk. Arrive at Black Hawk city limits in seven miles. Look left across Clear Creek to view the 1863 Lace House, a superb example of Carpenter Gothic architecture. Turn left on Colorado Highway 279 to enjoy the contiguous towns of Black Hawk-Central City National Historic District.

Central City is not large. It has narrow, curving streets. Park as soon as possible and get out and walk.

On Eureka Street find the best known buildings in town: the Teller House and the Opera House. U.S. Senator Henry Teller contributed to Central's fame by building the Teller House. Opened in 1872, it became the most famous hotel west of the Mississippi. When President Grant visited in 1873, he found the sidewalk fronting its entrance paved with silver bricks.

The most famous story about the Teller House concerns "The Face on the Barroom Floor." A sentimental ballad from the late 1800s tells of a derelict stumbling into a bar and sharing his tale of woe. His beautiful sweetheart had asked to meet a man whose portrait he was painting, and the two stole away together. The artist painted the lovely, but faithless, Madeline's picture on the saloon floor, then fell dead across it. Many legends surround the Teller House face, but she is not the original Madeline. This portrait dates from 1936.

Also famous, historically and artistically, the Central City Opera House reigns over the Little Kingdom. Originally opened in 1878, the theater features the mortarless stonework of Cornishmen, who arrived to work the smelters and the mines and became known as "Cousin Jacks." Boasting the best talent of the nation's theater in Central's boom days, the Opera House fell into disuse as mining dwindled. The dedicated work of the Central City Opera House Association culminated in the theater's reopening in 1932. On opening night Denver socialites arrived to enjoy Lillian Gish in the title role of *Camille*. The Opera House continues a summer schedule of operatic and theatrical productions, and players consider it a prestigious location in which to perform.

Explore Eureka and Main Streets to see buildings that are the oldest of their kind in Colorado. Find a variety of structures ranging from the jail and the Glory Hole to historic churches and homes.

George Pullman made enough money in Central to finance construction of his Pullman railroad cars. Here John B. Stetson came up with the hat that won the West. He believed that his wide-brimmed topper presented the best design for regional weather.

Retrace your route through Black Hawk to Highway 19 and back to Highway 6; then turn right. In four miles the road merges into Interstate 70 west. Drive three miles to Exit 241 and follow City Route 70 into Idaho Springs on Colorado Boulevard. After one mile bear left at the Central Business District sign.

At the Visitors Center find the larger-than-life statue of comic strip hero Steve Canyon. In 1947 some young World War II veterans decided that Idaho Springs needed publicity to attract more visitors. Their plan had two facets: one, to reach back into mining history and have an annual Gold Rush Days celebration; two, to memorialize their recent past and honor men who had fought for their country. The popularity of Milton Caniff's military cartoon characters led to the town's adoption of Steve Canyon.

Cross Clear Creek and look right to see old locomotive number 60 on a section of original tracks. After passing the engine, take the first one-way street right for one block and then turn left to follow Colorado out of town.

Continue on I-70 west twelve miles to Georgetown. Exit the Interstate, turn left under the highway and turn right at the stop sign. Go left over the bridge by the Guanella Pass sign and turn right into town.

Enter Georgetown on Rose Street. Pass City Park with its central gazebo and begin noticing well-preserved houses and churches. Drive as far as Sixth Street, look for a place to park and explore on foot. To your right find Visitors Information in the Courthouse/Community Center at Argentine Street; to your left, the Town Hall and Hotel de Paris beyond Taos Street.

The Hotel de Paris became the most notable star in the Silver Queen's crown. An enigmatic Frenchman named Louis Dupuy, injured when helping save a friend in a mine explosion, needed a calmer way to make a living. Beginning with a bakery and restaurant, Dupuy continued to enlarge and expand his operation. The resulting Hotel de Paris featured gourmet meals and a wine cellar to satisfy the most discriminating pallet. Imported art objects, fine furnishings and a 3,000-book library drew Dupuy's loyal patrons from far beyond Georgetown. His death in 1900 evoked a eulogy from the local newspaper: "Louis Dupuy—an eccentric, a philosopher and a student, who brought refinement to the granite slopes of Colorado."

Rising above Fifth Street, the Alpine Hose Company tower dominates Georgetown. During the Queen's boom days, five fire companies demonstrated their skills, even challenging other outfits to contests of ability with fire-fighting equipment. The Alpine Hose brought home first prize in the State Fireman's Tournament in both 1877 and 1879.

Walk past Grace Episcopal Church on Taos to reach Maxwell House to the left on Fourth. Walk or drive to Hammill House at Third and Argentine.

Maxwell House is a private home but you may enjoy the exterior of this dwelling, once honored as among the ten top examples of Victoriana in the nation. Hamill House opens as a museum, part of a five-home program to show everything from a miner's cabin to this historic mansion.

Silver speculator William A. Hammill's interests included building wagon roads, ranching and newspapers. He also remained active in state politics. The Hammill property includes the main house, carriage house and office building. And don't miss the fancy privy!

To reach the historic Georgetown Loop Railroad retrace your route back toward I-70 and follow the sign by the bridge. Even if you are not riding the train, drive up the road to view the remarkable high trestle. Surely "The Little Engine that Could" had nothing on the Georgetown Loop Railroad. Rails reached Georgetown in 1877, but not until 1884 did tracks arrive at the rich mining sites of Silver Plume, two miles away. The more than 600-foot change in altitude between the two towns created grades too steep for any train, and the narrow canyon disallowed switchbacks. An engineer's unique solution led to the Georgetown Loop. The track did indeed loop over itself as the Devil's Gate Viaduct trestle soared ninety-five feet above Clear Creek to cross the lower section of track and permit an acceptable grade for engines to pull.

Original success gave way to complete abandonment in 1939, when the high trestle brought $450 as scrap metal. By 1975, under the sponsorship of the Colorado Historical Society, the Georgetown Loop Railroad began hauling passengers once more; however, the trip remained incomplete without the high trestle. In 1982 the Boettcher Foundation contributed one million dollars. In 1984, one hundred years after rails first connected Georgetown and Silver Plume, a reconstructed Devil's Gate Viaduct bore trains once more.

The other end of the Georgetown Loop and the second portion of the Georgetown-Silver Plume Historic District, Silver Plume presents an interesting combination of ghost town elements and restoration. Reach the town by taking the next I-70 exit west of Georgetown. At the stop sign turn right over the bridge to explore Main Street both east and west. Note an old rooming house listing drunkenly, the abandoned school and ramshackle houses, along with spruced up, trim, restored homes.

Return to I-70 and continue west via the Eisenhower-Johnson Tunnel through the Continental Divide. Drive to Exit 203 and turn onto Colorado Highway 9 south, passing Lake Dillon.

Prospector Tom Dillon wouldn't believe his eyes if he were dropped into present-day Dillon. To this valley where the Blue and Snake Rivers and Ten Mile Creek flow together came Ute Indians, trappers and gold hopefuls. In the early 1960s came the flood as waters covered the old town of Dillon and created Dillon Reservoir.

Proceed on Highway 9 ten miles to Breckenridge. The gold camp acquired the name of John C. Breckinridge, vice president of the United States. The story goes that when Breckinridge opted for the Confederacy, indignant citizens kept the name but changed its spelling by deleting an "i" and adding an "e".

Breckenridge continues its Victorian heritage in the preservation of many historical buildings. Enjoy the picturesque shops on Main Street. East of Main find old homes and churches, particularly between Wellington and Washington on Ridge, French and Harris Streets. At Well-

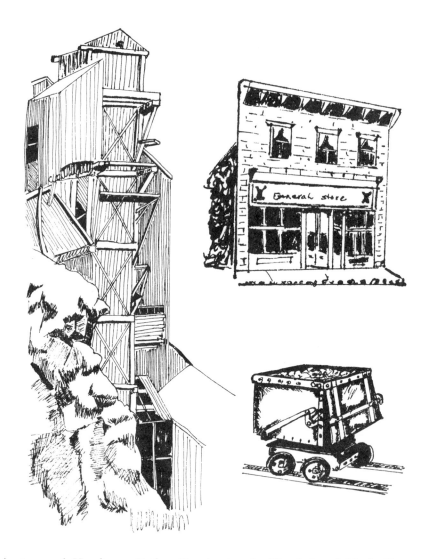

ington and Harris see Father Dyer's church. The beloved Methodist minister built Breckenridge's first church, carried the mail over the mountains, conducted widespread services, and wrote of his mining days' experiences in *The Snowshoe Itinerant.*

During the years from the end of World War II to the opening of Breckenridge Ski Area in 1961, the town flirted with "ghost" status. Now the combination of mining history and mountain snow combine to make Breckenridge one of Colorado's major ski resorts. It shares the spotlight with other Ski-the-Summit favorites such as Copper Mountain, Keystone and Arapahoe Basin. A-Basin boasts the highest ski area on the continent.

Complementing Summit County's winter treasures, Lake Dillon serves up summer aquatic treats. But then, Breckenridge has a nautical history dating back to the 1860s. "Captain" Sam Adams opined that boats launched on the Blue could navigate to the Pacific, and he organized the Breckenridge Navy. Unfortunately, the hard facts of geography did not cooperate with Adams' dream. Well, maybe old Cap'n Sam wasn't too far wrong; in 1984 a small yacht from Dillon appeared at a San Diego marina!

Continue through Breckenridge on Highway 9 over Hoosier Pass to Alma. Once located two miles away, the town of Buckskin Joe provided the story of a dancehall girl known as Silver Heels. Her habit of dancing in silver-heeled slippers delighted the miners and gave her this name. When a smallpox epidemic swept the town, she cared for the stricken miners, finally contracting the dread disease herself. Survivors raised money to thank Silver Heels for her unselfish devotion, but the disfigured dancer had disappeared. Mount Silverheels, near Alma, commemorates the heroism of the dancer turned nurse who, legend has it, returned as a heavily-veiled visitor to weep over the graves in Buckskin's cemetery.

Drive to Fairplay, once the business center to South Park's ranching and mining. Try not to rush through town on your way back, since several points of interest command attention. For example, Park County claims the oldest continuously operating courthouse in Colorado.

Turn right on Fourth Street to South Park City, central focus of Fairplay's offerings. The museum presents a composite old mining town with buildings from Alma, Fairplay and other sites. Created in 1959 to celebrate the Rush to the Rockies centennial, South Park City features dwellings ranging from cabin to homestead to pioneer home. Structures such as brewery, bank and stagecoach inn represent the business community. Professional displays include doctor's and dentist's offices and drug store. To complete the picture, add mining, transportation, social, and education units.

On Front Street between Fifth and Sixth, a memorial on the right commemorates the faithful and necessary service of burros to miners as it salutes Prunes, who lived from 1867 to 1930 and worked all the mines in Alma and Fairplay. Another tribute to the "Rocky Mountain Canaries" comes with the annual World Championship Pack Burro race.

Turn left on Sixth and two blocks ahead see the 1874 Sheldon Jackson Memorial Church, a small, Gothic, white frame structure.

Leave Fairplay via Highway 9 south. You will see piles of rock left from the gold dredging operations after 9 separates from Highway 285. Continue on 9 to US Highway 24 and turn left for seventy miles to reach downtown Colorado Springs.

LEADVILLE

Scientists researching high altitude reactions find that a person's capacity to work declines about three percent for each 1,000 feet. If you feel as though you'd been sprinkled with "goofy dust," remember that Leadville claims the honor of being the nation's highest incorporated city. Climax, at the top of Fremont Pass, boasts the country's highest post office.

In both its silver mining past and its molybdenum mining present Leadville has experienced crippling slumps. The 1980s answer was to revitalize the business district by means of "Operation Bootstrap." Red brick sidewalks, refurbished buildings and a variety of entertainment dress up the Cloud City's mixture of old and new. An annual community celebration, the August Boom Days, includes burro races and rock drilling contests.

The Leadville tour occurs geographically between the trip to Cripple Creek and that to Aspen. If you have more than one day, you can add on Leadville after Florissant from the Cripple Creek tour or continue to Aspen from Twin Lakes on the Leadville tour.

Mileage: 300 miles   *Actual driving time: 6 hours*

Leadville's altitude, fabulous mining treasures and colorful characters combine to give this National Historic Landmark a superlative history. Located at 10,152 feet, the Cloud City became the world's richest silver producer and unearthed its largest variety of mined products: gold, silver, zinc, lead, tungsten, tin, molybdenum, and turquoise. It also sheltered people like H.A.W. Tabor and the Unsinkable Molly Brown.

Gold began the Leadville story in 1860 with prospectors panning near the headwaters of the Arkansas River. One of these explorers announced to his companions: "I've got all of California in this here pan!" The site became known as California Gulch and the shanty mining town as Oro City. As usual in Colorado placer mining, deposits played out fairly quickly, and most miners drifted toward new strikes. Those remaining worked the streams with sluices and Long Toms, grumbling about the heavy black sand that clogged their efforts.

In the mid-1870s two men who knew their mining suspected that the "worthless" black rock from which the sand came might be hiding a new bonanza. Assays revealed black lead carbonate, rich in silver. One year after its 1878 incorporation date, Leadville had become a city with the usual mining town inventory of saloons, red light district and crime. Population continued to escalate; law, order and capitalism followed. The Tabor Opera House and the Clarendon Hotel added a touch of culture and refinement.

H.A.W. Tabor, a shopkeeper in both Oro City and Leadville, staked two miners to provisions in exchange for one-third interest if they found ore. The resulting Little Pittsburg discovery began Tabor's rise to fortune. The "salted"

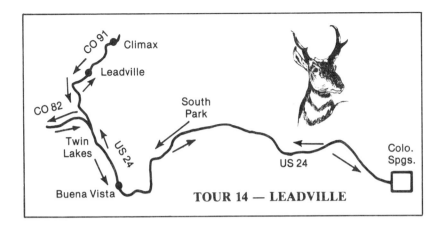

TOUR 14 — LEADVILLE

Chrysolite Mine revealed a rich lode. The Matchless Mine parlayed a $117,000 investment into a $100,000 a month return. Tabor went on to become the richest man in Colorado, lieutenant governor of the state and United States Senator, filling the term of Henry Teller, who moved on to President Arthur's Cabinet. Tabor also divorced his first wife, beloved in the mining district, to marry the beautiful, young Baby Doe. He finally lost his entire fortune in the Crash of 1893.

The history of the old mining towns is exciting enough without any embellishments, but wonderful legends attach themselves like barnacles and became part of folklore if not of fact. For example, one-time Leadville resident Mrs. J. J. Brown (the Unsinkable Molly) attracted her share. One popular story tells how "Leadville Johnny" Brown brought home a stack of thousand dollar bills and told Molly to hide it away somewhere. She chose the safest place she could think of, but when Johnny came home late and lit a fire in the stove, $300,000 went up in smoke. Johnny laughed and told Molly he'd make that back and more — and he did!

Leadville's history is full of other famous Colorado names. David Moffat's millions built Colorado railroads. David May sold dry goods and went on to establish the May Company department stores. Charles Boettcher began a hardware business here, created his own financial empire and figured prominently in the history of Denver.

The 1893 Crash reduced Leadville's silver mines from eighty to eighteen. But the earth still yielded gold and zinc and lead — with new surprises just around the corner. To shore up the gloom, city fathers opted for a spectacular grandstand play in 1895 and voted to build history's biggest, most dazzling Ice Palace. Ice blocks came from as far away as Palmer Lake to provide the 5,000 tons required to construct a huge, Norman-style fortress. Two corner towers thrust their battlements ninety feet into the air, and a 19-foot ice statue of Lady Leadville on a 12-foot pedestal stretched out her right arm toward the ore-rich hills. Within the five-acre colossus visitors enjoyed ice skating and curling rinks, as well as a heated dining room and ballroom. Before its January 1, 1896, grand opening a balmy December chinook wind threatened the structure and a record-breaking, early, warm spring led to its closing before the end of March.

Although a whole mountain of it had been discovered near Leadville in 1879 and Colorado School of Mines labs identified it in 1900, no one knew what to do with molybdenum until World War I. Then European sources reported that Germany used the mineral to harden steel in Krupp's Big Bertha cannons. Military necessities of two world wars and other conflicts turned "moly" mining into a twentieth-century boom. Atop Fremont Pass, once the highest station on the Denver and Rio Grande Western Railroad, lies the Climax Molybdenum Mine, largest in the Free World. When steel bottomed out in the early 1980s, Climax closed down for eighteen months, throwing Leadville into a slump worse than that of the 1890s. Bouncing back again, the moly mine reopened in 1984.

Colorado's two tallest peaks, Mount Elbert and Mount Massive, guard Leadville. To the east Mosquito Pass, at 13,188 feet, remains the most elevated mountain crossing in North America. Leadville claims the country's highest airport, college campus and golf course. Follow Highway 24 through South Park, to Buena Vista, and along the Arkansas to this city of superlatives.

Begin this tour by driving west from Colorado Springs on US Highway 24. Continue past Florissant to the town of Lake George; cross the South Platte River and ascend 9,507-foot Wilkerson Pass. South Park stretches out before you toward the peaks of the Continental Divide.

South Park ranks second only to the San Luis Valley in the list of Colorado's four intermontane parks and surpasses both Middle and North Parks in size. Mountain men prized the busy beaver ponds and meadows of the upland plains. Indians valued South Park as a hunting ground with vast herds of buffalo, pronghorn and elk. Even today visitors spot pronghorn herds.

Samuel Hartsel of Pennsylvania gave his name to the small community west of South Park. Hartsel came for gold but found success in sales of cattle to the "go backs," those retreating from futile mining efforts. Hartsel gets credit for beginning South Park's ranching, and the town became an important junction in mining days.

Proceed west on Highway 24 over Trout Creek Pass (8,488 feet) to Buena Vista (Spanish "good view"), ninety miles west of Colorado Springs at the confluence of the Arkansas River and Cottonwood Creek. Note a state correctional facility for juveniles east of town on the right.

Just as cowboys let off steam in competitions that became rodeos, so also did miners make recreational use of their most familiar animals, and pack burro racing resulted. This unique sport involves a burro with pack accompanied by a human companion who runs beside the animal for as far as thirty miles and to altitudes over 12,000 feet. Each summer Buena Vista joins Leadville and Fairplay in hosting the Triple Crown of burro racing.

Find Buena Vista's Visitors Center on your right at Highway 24 and

Mill Street. Billing itself as "The Whitewater Capital of the County," the town serves as a good jumping off place for outdoor activities: fishing, hunting, exploring ghost towns, hiking, camping, climbing, and, of course, rafting. Visit Buena Vista's colorful and compact downtown by turning right at the traffic light on Main. As it did in mining days, the community makes a convenient stopping place on the way to Leadville.

Drive north from Buena Vista on Highway 24 with the Sawatch Mountains crowding in on your left. Along this "Highway of the Fourteeners," both north and south of Buena Vista, rise about one-fourth of Colorado's 14,000-foot mountains. Included in the "good view" find the Collegiate Range of Mounts Princeton, Yale, Columbia, Harvard, and Oxford. Note that the mountains are named from south to north just as the colleges are located geographically. Pass Mount Elbert, highest peak in Colorado, and Mount Massive, second highest.

The Arkansas River accompanies you on the right. This river route to Leadville occasioned the "Royal Gorge War" between the rival Denver and Rio Grande and Santa Fe railroads.

Fifteen miles north of Buena Vista, two signs on the right relate to transportation. One points out the old stage road to Leadville. The other describes the difficulties encountered as men sought to roll everything from wagons to trains across tough mountain terrain. Railroad builders chose a narrow gauge track, only three feet wide, to cut construction costs.

Highway 24 reaches Stringtown, then continues to Leadville roughly paralleling California Gulch where prospectors originally discovered gold. Enter downtown on Harrison Street and find a concentration of the Cloud City's interesting locales from Third to Tenth Streets.

Between Third and Fourth on the right note the Tabor Opera House. Opened in 1879, the $35,000 building welcomed patrons into its plush red and gold, gas-lighted interior and hosted internationally famous performers. The Clarendon Hotel stood next door until the 1930s. Look about half way back on the right side of the Opera House to a window with an iron grillwork balcony. At this point a walkway connected the two buildings so that Haw and Baby Doe Tabor could proceed directly from the theater to their hotel suite.

The next four attractions lie east or west of Harrison. In each case turn right or left as indicated, then return to Harrison to continue the tour.

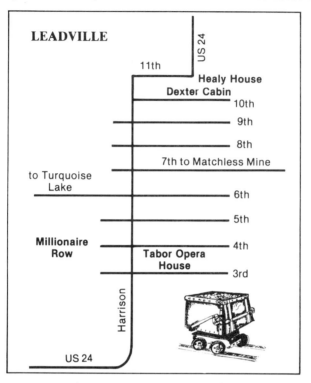

Left on Fourth discover vestiges of Millionaires' Row. Although not as lavish as one might expect, the Row preserves some lovingly restored Victorian homes. Note the "House with the Eye" at 127 West Fourth. The structure takes its name from the eyelid dormer window enclosing a stained glass eye.

Right on Fifth at No. 116 discover the modest 1877 home of Haw and Augusta Tabor before he became a multi-millionaire and turned to Baby Doe.

To reach Turquoise Lake Recreation Area, less than six miles away, turn left on Sixth until it deadends, turn right and bear left at the first fork. Mountain forests surround the man-made storage reservoir, and the Sawatch Mountains provide its backdrop. The area honors famous Leadville citizens in such titles as Baby Doe and Molly Brown Campgrounds and Tabor boat ramp.

Turn right on Seventh for more than one mile to reach Haw Tabor's Matchless Mine and the shack where Baby Doe ended her tragic last years. On the way pass the old railroad station and engine to the left at Hazel Street. The road beyond the Matchless continues to Mosquito Pass. As men sought a suitable name for the high crossing, they found a dead mosquito between the pages of a book.

At Eighth and Harrison on the left see the Arts and Humanities Center. Enjoy a multi-media presentation, "The Earth Runs Silver: Early Leadville." Beyond the Center and set back from the street find Visitors Information. At Ninth and Harrison the Heritage Museum and Gallery occupies a former Carnegie Library.

Although Highway 24 turns right at Ninth, the tour continues straight ahead to Tenth and visits two Colorado Historical Society properties, Healy House and Dexter Cabin. A mining engineer built the 1878 Healy House. Today, role-playing, costumed guides help its history come alive. You're in for a surprise when you enter the cabin; it's no rough miner's pad! *(These attractions are open only between Memorial Day and Labor Day.)*

Turn right on Eleventh for one block, then turn left and follow Highway 24 to its junction with Colorado Highway 91. The tour continues on 91, but Highway 24 heads up Tennessee Pass where events of World War II wrote a twentieth-century chapter in Leadville's story. The Tenth Mountain Division trained on top of the pass at legendary Camp Hale. Recruits arrived from Camp Carson in Colorado Springs to undergo rigorous training in skiing and mountaineering skills. Officers eventually declared bawdy Leadville off limits, so troops enjoyed leave time in Aspen. Veterans of the Tenth, having earned their glory in the mountains of Italy, returned to launch the ski industry in the mountains of Colorado.

Follow Highway 91 twelve miles north to Climax Molybdenum Company, a division of AMAX, Inc. Here rests the world's largest known molybdenite deposit. The silver-gray metal's weight resembles lead but with a very high melting point. Most moly mined throughout the world becomes a strengthener for other metals, particularly steels. The huge Climax mine works both open pit and underground with the capacity to produce 48,000 tons of ore per day. From the mine the moly ore moves to ball mills for grinding and to flotation cells for recovery of the metal.

Return to Leadville and drive south on Highway 24 to Colorado Highway 82. Watch for a difference in the Arkansas River north and south of this intersection. The river arrives from the north as a young mountain stream. Leaving the power plant, the waters rush and surge to the south.

Turn right on Highway 82 and drive four miles to visit the Mount Elbert Powerplant at Twin Lakes. Like Grand Lake, Twin Lakes owe their origin to glacial activity. The natural bodies of water boast fourteen miles of shoreline at a 9,200-foot elevation. When the Fryingpan-Arkansas diversion project began, engineers enlarged Twin Lakes for more storage capacity. The powerplant receives water via a conduit from Turquoise Lake and transmits it to the Arkansas River. Over 69,000 acre-feet of water each year pass from the Fryingpan Basin to the Eastern

Slope. The Visitors Center at the powerplant presents a wealth of displays on the water diversion project and points of interest.

Buildings visible across the lake opposite the plant reflect the site of Interlaken Resort, active until 1890. One percent of the money invested in the Fryingpan-Arkansas project went toward restoration of the properties, now Interlaken National Historic District. An entertaining tale out of Leadville's boom days tells of plans to procure Venetian-type gondolas to ply the lakes. When queried about how many to purchase, a miner of newly acquired wealth but limited literacy replied, "Aw, just buy two of 'em and let 'em breed"!

Retrace your route back to Highway 24 and go right to return to Colorado Springs.

CRIPPLE CREEK

To round out this book of driving tours, we have come full circle and returned to the Pikes Peak Region. The final tour explores Manitou Springs, Ute Pass, the Cripple Creek Mining District, and Florissant Fossil Beds National Monument. Summer in Cripple Creek brings the Imperial Hotel's Victorian Theatre, more popularly known as melodrama. See the descendants of the miners' burros and enjoy the annual Donkey Derby Days. Ride a steam-driven, narrow gauge train to the old mines. This is also a popular trip for fall aspen viewing, and its proximity to Colorado Springs provides year-round accessibility.

Mileage: 115 miles   *Actual driving time: 3 hours*

Gold in Cripple Creek? Nobody believed cowboy prospector Bob Womack when he passed the word in the Colorado City saloons. The discoverer of the soon-to-be bonanza was "in his cups" much too often, and his fellow drinkers chalked it up to another of Bob's fanciful tales. Besides, there had been the Mt. Pisgah hoax, during which fake "salted" mines on the conical hill west of the present town brought the usual flurry of goldseekers and their hangers-on, following a wild goose chase. What's more, everyone knew you didn't look for gold in the granite crater of an extinct volcano 9,600 feet high; Colorado gold sheltered in quartz outcroppings, easy to see and trace.

Gold in Cripple Creek! Unlikely, unbelievable, but true! Here the precious metal combined in a distinctive purplish-colored rock formation called sylvanite or calaverite — a gold, silver and tellurium mixture. Another surprise revealed that the ore became richer as the veins deepened. In 1874 a member of the official Hayden Geological and Geographical Survey first discovered goldbearing "float," ore pieces weathered or broken off from the parent rock. Womack made a similar find in 1878 but did not stake his initial claim until 1886. His 1890 discovery of the El Paso Lode in Poverty Gulch put Cripple Creek on the map.

The Welty family homesteaded and ranched in the region beginning in 1871. Accidents to people and/or animals around the area's small stream produced the name Cripple Creek. Denver realtors Horace Bennett and Julius Myers acquired acreage in 1885, planning to promote hunting and fishing amid the beautiful mountain scenery. Instead, they turned into millionaire developers.

Although only three producing mines operated in 1891, it was a portentous year for the new gold camp. Prospectors christened it the Cripple Creek Mining District. Colorado Springs carpenter Winfield Scott Stratton staked claim to his treasure chest, the Independence Mine, on July 4. Broadmoor's Count James Pourtales provided noble sanction by investing in a mine. Bennett and Myers platted their town, choosing to keep the name Cripple Creek.

The world-wide depression in the early 1890s also touched Cripple Creek. The United States abandoned bimetallism and adopted the gold standard, depressing

117

Colorado's favorite crop, silver, and pushing unemployed miners to the new District. Along with the influx of workers came severe, and sometimes violent, labor problems and strikes, the first beginning in 1893 and not settled until the following year.

This settlement released energies for peaceful development and preceded the finest years of the District's boom. Cripple Creek and Victor headed the list of more than fifteen mining communities. The Florence and Cripple Creek Railroad arrived from the south, beating out the Midland Terminal line from the north. On December 15, 1895, the *Morning Times* urged its readers to "go to church and thank the Giver of all good things for guiding your footsteps to Cripple Creek."

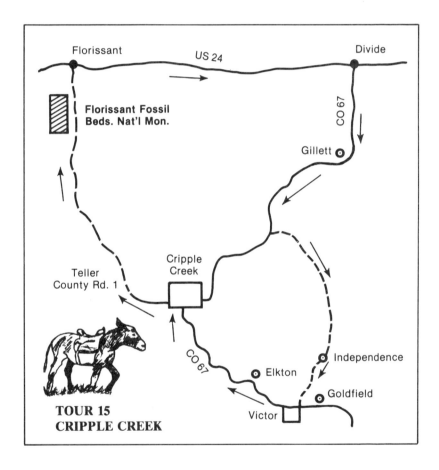

The jerry-built society of ramshackle wooden buildings heard the dreaded fire alarm on April 25, 1896. An entertainer and her companion had upset a stove as they quarreled. The following day the *Denver Republican* headlines read: "Jennie LaRue Goes into History with the Chicago Kicker." Scant days later, on April 29, a second conflagration, apparently ignited in a hotel service area, destroyed most of the remaining parts of town.

Rising from the ashes, rebuilding began quickly, with modern brick and stone structures replacing the vulnerable wooden buildings. Cripple Creek gained the status of county seat for newly-created Teller County. Gold production increased, with 475 producing mines operating during the peak years of 1899-1902. The "Short Line" railroad traveled from Colorado Springs through views so spectacular that they prompted Teddy Roosevelt to call the ride "the trip that bankrupts the English language."

Cripple Creek produced an enviable collection of mining millionaires, but financial success came also to those who "mined the miners." For example, A.E. "Bert" Carlton amassed a fortune by cornering the freight market and monopolizing the reduction mill business.

The most recent mining discovery came in 1914 with the unearthing of the Cresson Vug, a gold-bedecked cavern resembling an enormous geode. The Cresson find and the Carlton Tunnel, constructed to drain off water from the lower levels of the older mines, provided the last shots in the arm to an ailing economy. A virtual death blow struck with World War I. Mines closed as young men went off to war, and houses disappeared as war needs demanded lumber. Following the Armistice, the worldwide influenza epidemic, which seemed to flourish in high altitudes, attacked the District with a particular virulence.

The 1920s and 30s saw Cripple Creek as one of Colorado's near ghost towns. During the 1940s a happy renaissance began, sparked by Dorothy and Wayne Mackin, who revived the failing Imperial Hotel. The success story continues to this day.

Begin this tour by driving west from downtown Colorado Springs on Midland Expressway. In seven miles exit to Manitou Springs.

Many Colorado cities include the word "springs" in their name. In the case of Colorado Springs no natural waters exist, but generally the title reflects the presence of underground bubblings. Manitou Springs features both soda and iron springs, familiar to Indians, mountain men, settlers, and tourists for their therapeutic value. Originally known simply as Manitou, the spa hosted health seekers who arrived from nationwide and abroad to "take the waters." Those not fortunate enough to make the journey could partake of the healing liquids widely dispensed by local bottling works.

Enter the town on Manitou Avenue and find the Chamber of Commerce on your right at Mayfair Avenue. Across Mayfair locate Briarhurst, the "little English cottage" that housed Dr. and Mrs. William A. Bell and their family. British Dr. Bell joined General Palmer in developing the Pikes Peak Region.

If you plan a full day for this tour, you will have time for a stop in Manitou Springs to explore historic sites and interesting shops. Old churches, homes and commercial buildings share acreage with boutiques and artists' wares. From the Y at Wheeler Clock you can enjoy Manitou and Canon Avenues. At the west end of town Ruxton Avenue bears left to reach Miramont Castle and the start of both the Pikes Peak Cog Railway and the Mt. Manitou Incline.

The tour continues through town on Highway 24 to reach Ute Pass, ancient highway of the Blue Sky People. Reach Cascade and turn left, following the signs for the Pikes Peak Highway. Visit three small Ute Pass communities before rejoining Highway 24 west. In Cascade find the Ute Pass Museum and note the turnoff for the Peak road and Santa's Workshop.

Jolly old St. Nick and his helpers reside at Santa's Workshop, North Pole, Pikes Peak. Rides, shops and friendly animals highlight the mountainside village with its storybook buildings.

Pikes Peak, one of America's most famous mountains, has endured a variety of ascents since Zebulon Pike's 1806 pronouncement that "no human being could have ascended to its pinical." Auto racers tackle its slopes each summer for the Pikes Peak Hillclimb. Runners make the round trip to the summit in the Pikes Peak Marathon competition. At year's end the AdAmAn Club hikes the trail to the top and sets off fireworks at midnight on New Year's Eve. And yearly, thousands of tourists and residents drive twenty miles to the 14,110-foot summit.

Follow the main road with the center yellow line from Cascade through Chipeta Park to reach Green Mountain Falls. All three towns served as mountain resorts and each had its own festive hotel, since lost to fire. Colorado Midland trains delivered visitors for vacation stays or day excursions.

Pass the lake at Green Mountain Falls, with its 1888 gazebo. See the Church in the Wildwood on the left.

You may choose to take short, interesting detours up the hill to the left to view vintage cottages or to go straight ahead on Belvidere past the House of the Seven Gables and other historic properties until the road deadends by a trail to the falls.

The tour turns right over the bridge and up the hill to meet Highway 24 west. Pass through Woodland Park, one of the fastest growing communities in Colorado, and reach Divide. At this former railroad junction, the Midland Terminal Railway headed south to the Cripple Creek Mining District. Turn left and follow the old railroad bed to the site of the last major precious metal strike in Colorado.

State Highway 67 takes you through ranching and resort country, by hillsides of aspen, past the west side of Pikes Peak, and through a one-lane tunnel, vestige of the Midland Terminal. In thirteen miles one road goes straight ahead to Victor, but the tour turns right toward Cripple Creek. At this fork, on the right, stood the town of Gillett, site of the only true Spanish-style bullfight ever staged in the United States. Humane Society authorities prevented a repetition of the first spectacle.

After the ruins of Gillett you will begin passing evidence of mining days' diggings before you reach the spectacular overview of Cripple Creek. Nestled in the bowl of an extinct volcano, with the majestic Sangre de Cristos as a backdrop, the one-time world's richest gold camp evokes many a memory of its glorious past.

The history of Cripple Creek gold began when volcanic forces caused molten lava to push through the thick cover of Pikes Peak granite. The resulting channels carried liquid, ore-bearing magma which fanned out into fissures near the surface. This geologic process explains why ore veins became richer as mine shafts extended underground and prompted Winfield Scott Stratton's "bowl of gold" theory. Stratton speculated that all the veins ran together, as though at the bottom of a giant goblet, to form a reservoir of gold.

Continue toward Cripple Creek until you reach the Molly Kathleen. Just before the mine turn left uphill on a dirt road for the five-mile trip to Victor. Go to the yield sign, bear right to the Y and take the left fork (the right fork will be marked Range View Road). Drive through the valley to reach another fork and turn right.

After you circle the hillside, look for abandoned mines and the picturesque, weathered buildings that once comprised the town of Independence. Complete the short distance to the intersection with Range View Road and turn left. As you descend the hill, look left to see the large, circular, concrete structures that held explosives used in mining operations. Across the highway stands Goldfield town, once third largest in the District.

At the bottom of Range View, turn left for one-quarter mile to the Y formed by Highway 67 and Teller County Road 44. Pull into the triangle between the two roads and look back up Battle Mountain to some of the legendary giants of the Cripple Creek Mining District: the Strong, Independence, Portland, and Ajax Mines.

Return to Victor on Highway 67. Turn left on Third by the Business District sign, and drive one block to Victor Avenue. Diagonally across the street find the Victor - Lowell Thomas Museum. The famous newsman, whose father was a town doctor, graduated from Victor High School.

Turn right on Victor Avenue and continue to the old City Hall on the right. Stop here to absorb some information about the fabled mining days from the adjacent billboard. Note that the District's production totaled $800 million, mined by 6,000 miners who received a combined monthly payroll of $650,000.

Continue out of Victor on Highway 67 for the five-mile drive to Cripple Creek. One mile out of town, around a sharp curve, look right to see the ruins of Elkton. In another mile see the Carlton Mill on the left. Watch for the little narrow gauge train that steams out of Cripple Creek. Enter Cripple Creek and turn right on Myers Avenue, a dirt road that is one block before the main street of buildings.

Myers Avenue lived up to its reputation as the most notorious red light district in America. Of the original parlour houses, however, only the Old Homestead Museum remains. In its heyday the Homestead reigned over Myers Avenue. The death of its most famous madame, the elegant Pearl DeVere, prompted a colorful funeral procession to the cemetery on Mt. Pisgah.

Drive to the end of Myers, go left for one block and turn right onto Bennett Avenue. Proceed to the former railroad depot, one of the few buildings to survive the 1896 fires, now home to the Cripple Creek District Museum. Several other attractions cluster in the vicinity, including the station for the Cripple Creek and Victor Railroad.

From the museum start back along Bennett Avenue. The dramatic difference in elevation between one side of the street and the other gives credence to an old Cripple Creek joke: "A man broke his leg (or neck) last night falling off Bennett Avenue"! In two blocks the Imperial Hotel stands to the right up the hill. Anchoring revitalized Cripple Creek, the Imperial's excellent Victorian Theatre draws crowds during the summer season. The Gold Bar Room provides the setting for a melodramatic, nineteenth-century play and the Olio.

Along Bennett find sturdy brick and stone buildings constructed after the two disastrous fires. Imagine what it must have been like when 50,000 people thronged the District and thousands of mine shafts pockmarked the hills for six square miles.

Continue on Bennett until you must turn right; drive one block and turn left, following the directions to Mt. Pisgah. Taking the name of the Biblical height from which Moses viewed the Promised Land, Mt. Pisgah is the cone-shaped hill to the left. A drive to the top provides a 360-degree view of the volcanic bowl and the surrounding mountains. Also on the hill locate Cripple's cemetery.

Follow well-maintained, dirt Teller County Road 1. When a choice of roads occurs at Evergreen Station, drive straight ahead past massive rock formations.

Fourteen miles from Cripple Creek reach the sign for Florissant Fossil Beds National Monument. In two more miles turn left opposite the red barn to reach the Visitors Center. Learn how volcanic ash trapped plants and insects, then turned to rock containing carbon imprints of these organisms. Fossil finds in the shale layers indicate that sequoias, ferns, palms, and magnolias, plus countless subtropical insects, lived in this valley 35 million years ago. Scientists also have discovered every fossil

butterfly in the New World. Displays at the center and a short nature trail introduce both ancient fossils and today's natural history. Florissant means "flowering" in French; enjoy Colorado's seasonal wildflowers.

Turn left out of the National Monument entrance. Within one mile note the Historic Site sign and turn left into the Hornbek Homestead. Typical of the region's 160-acre parcels, the property features dwellings, barns and sheds, as well as a root-cellar on the hillside to the right. Its uniqueness stems from the fact that a woman filed the homesteading claim in 1878. As time and money allow, restoration continues on the homestead.

Proceed north on Teller County 1 two miles to Highway 24 and turn right. Four miles east of Florissant uprooted trees on the hillside give evidence of a tornado's passing in the early 1980s, a rare happening for these parts. Drive another thirty-four miles to reach downtown Colorado Springs.

A COLORADO READING LIST

Not a formal bibliography, this list contains suggestions for further reading about the parts of Colorado included on the tours. Some sources provided background material for TRIPS ON WHEELS; others simply provided enjoyable vehicles for further exploration and education.

Abbott, Carl, Stephen J. Leonard and David McComb *Colorado*
Brown, Robert L. *Ghost Towns of the Colorado Rockies*
Collins, Dabney Otis *Land of Tall Skies*
Crofutt's *Grip-Sack Guide of Colorado*, 1885 Edition
Dallas, Sandra *Gaslights and Gingerbread*
Fetler, John *The Pikes Peak People*
Fowler, Gene *A Solo in Tom-Toms*
                Timber Line
Freed, Elaine, and David Barber *Historic Sites and Structures El Paso County, Colorado*
Hart, John L. Jerome *Fourteen Thousand Feet*
Howbert, Irving *Indians of the Pikes Peak Region*
                Memories of a Lifetime in the Pikes Peak Region
Karsner, David *Silver Dollar, A Story of the Tabors*
Le Compte, Janet *Pueblo, Hardscrabble, and Greenhorn*
Lee, Mabel Barbee *Back in Cripple Creek*
                Cripple Creek Days
Lowie, Robert H. *Indians of the Plains*
Mutel, Cornelia Fleisher and John C. Emerick *From Grassland to Glacier — The Natural History of Colorado*
Pearl, Richard M. *America's Mountain: Pikes Peak*
Shubert, Frank N. *Vanguard of Expansion: Army Engineers in the Trans-Mississippi West, 1819-1879*
Simmons, Virginia McConnell *The San Luis Valley: Land of the Six-Armed Cross*
Sprague, Marshall *Colorado*
                Money Mountain
                Newport in the Rockies
Turk, Gayle *Trial and Triumph*
                Wet Mountain Valley
Ubbelohde, Carl, Maxine Benson, and Duane A. Smith *A Colorado History*
Waters, Frank *Midas of the Rockies*
Wolle, Muriel Sibell *Stampede to Timberline*
WPA Writers' Program *Colorado — A Guide to the Highest State*

Transcripts of Speeches
The Honorable Oscar L. Chapman, Secretary of the Interior, at the Seventy-Fifth Anniversary of Statehood, 1951, "Colorado — The Growth of the Mountain State"
Dr. William F. Slocum, former President of The Colorado College, Sept. 1, 1929, at the Dedication of the Memorial Statue of General William J. Palmer

See TRIPS ON TWOS for detailed information on Colorado Springs, the United States Air Force Academy and Manitou Springs.

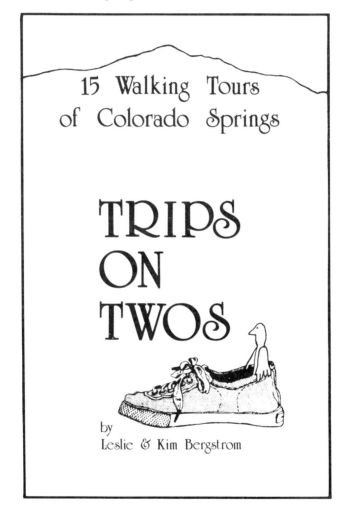

15 Walking Tours
of Colorado Springs

TRIPS
ON
TWOS

by
Leslie & Kim Bergstrom

ABOUT THE AUTHOR

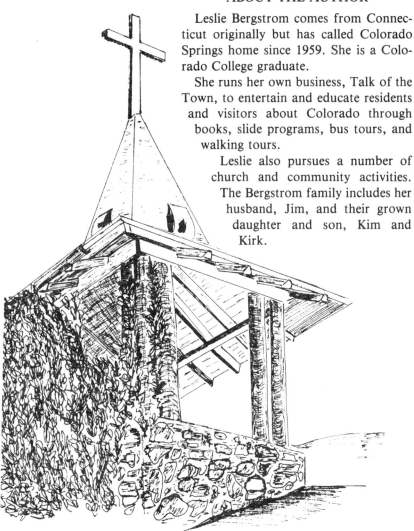

Leslie Bergstrom comes from Connecticut originally but has called Colorado Springs home since 1959. She is a Colorado College graduate.

She runs her own business, Talk of the Town, to entertain and educate residents and visitors about Colorado through books, slide programs, bus tours, and walking tours.

Leslie also pursues a number of church and community activities. The Bergstrom family includes her husband, Jim, and their grown daughter and son, Kim and Kirk.

ABOUT THE ARTIST

Cyndy Wacker is a free-lance artist residing in Colorado Springs with her husband and four children.

She was raised and educated in Nebraska, then spent seven years traveling with her husband, Tom, who was in the United States Navy. The family has lived in Colorado since 1977.

Besides her permanent job of homemaker and mother to Jennifer, Trisha, Scott, and Sarah, Cyndy is busy with her church and volunteer activities. Her art work is a source of pleasure and relaxation.

Thank you for making TRIPS ON WHEELS *your travel guide. It has been a labor of love to research, prepare and present these fifteen driving tours and a delight to have you along as companions!*

NOTES